REPLACEMENT CHILD

A memoir
By
Judy L. Mandel

Some names and identifying details of people described in this book have been changed to protect their privacy. This is a work of memory, and at times imagination, based on the true story of the plane crash depicted in the book and the author's life experience. The essential facts of the story are true.

Library of Congress Control Number: 2009906784

ISBN 9780982514603

www.schlesingerbooks.com
www.replacementchild.com
www.judymandel.com

This book is dedicated to the memory of my sisters:
Linda Sue (Mandel) Driskell,
the bravest woman I ever knew
who taught me that anything can be overcome,
and
Donna Jo Mandel,
who I wish I had known in life.

And, in memory of my parents:
Albert Alexander Mandel
and
Florence Margaret (Schlesinger) Mandel.
My heroes.

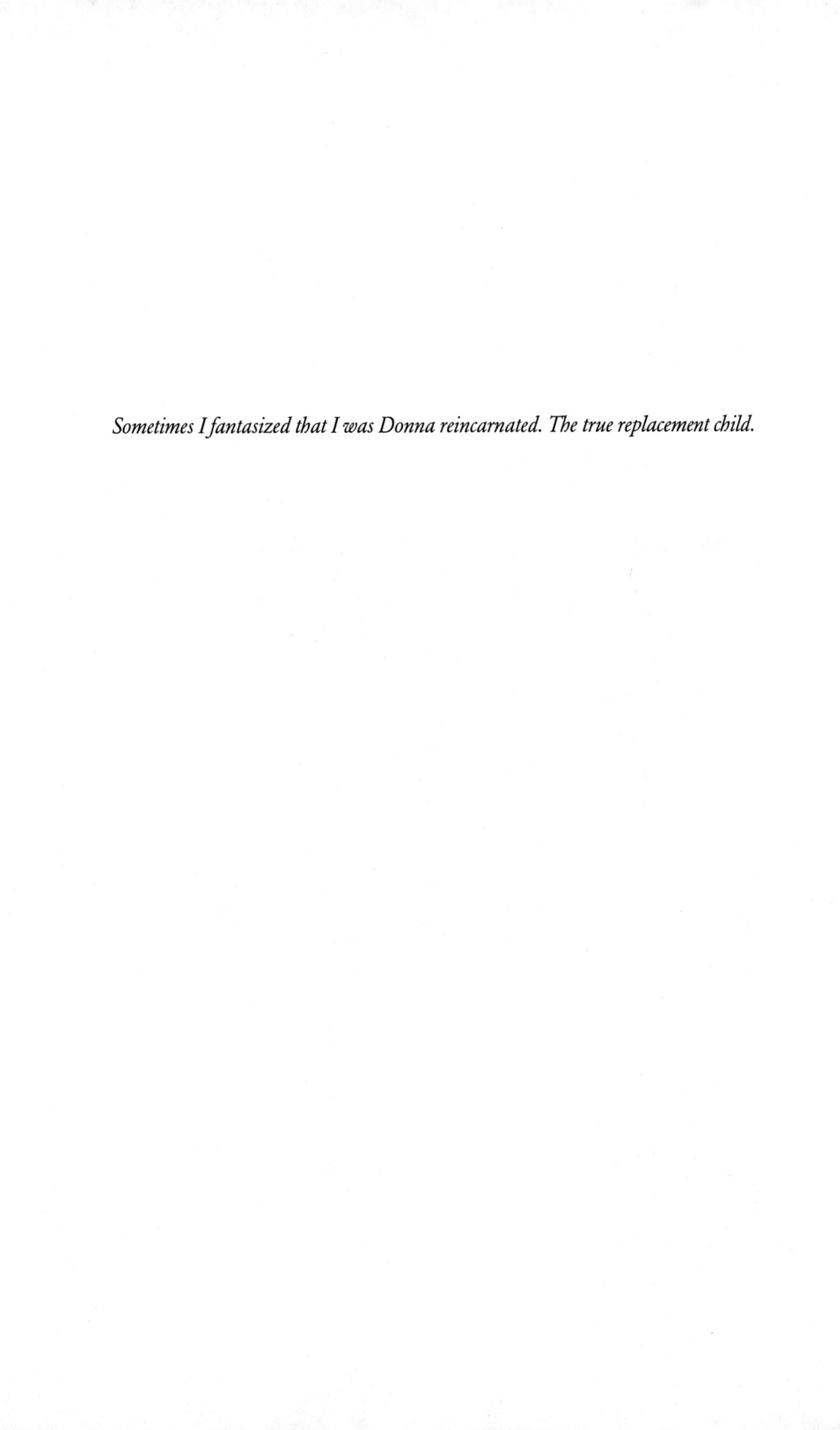

Sometimes I fantasized that I was Donna reincarnated. The true replacement child.

Excerpt:

ELIZABETH DAILY JOURNAL

WEDNESDAY, JANUARY 23, 1952

28 PERISH IN AIRLINER'S FALL ON WILLIAMSON STREET HOMES...

ELIZABETH, N.J. – Elizabeth's second aviation holocaust in thirty-seven days today had claimed at least twenty-eight lives... The ship plunged into the two houses near the southeast corner of South and Williamson streets at approximately 3:43 P.M. Before firemen could subdue the roaring, orange flames that leaped nearly 100 feet into the rainy sky, three dwellings and a garage had been destroyed and a fourth house was damaged severely. Nearly a score of persons were homeless.

Killed on the plane were Captain (Thomas J.) Reid and all twenty-two others aboard. Police... announced the following list of Elizabeth persons missing and feared dead:

DONNA MANDEL, 7 years old, 310 Williamson Street...

The hospitalized Elizabethians and their condition at 8 o'clock this morning at St. Elizabeth Hospital:

LINDA MANDEL, 2 ½, of 310 Williamson Street, "poor."

MRS. FLORENCE MANDEL, 35, her mother, shock and burns of both hands, "fairly good."

... Mrs. Mandel picked up Linda, her clothes afire, and rolled her down the stairway to the street, her husband Albert Mandel said. Mrs. Mandel, her own garments ignited, attempted to struggle back into the house to seek Donna but was restrained by an unidentified man.

Prologue

I was born of fire.

The flames licked my mother's kitchen clean.

It happened at 3:45 pm on a foggy winter afternoon – January 22, 1952.

The American Airlines Flight 6780 that crashed into my parents' home at 310 Williamson Street was the second of three crashes in Elizabeth, New Jersey within three months. Newark Airport was just three miles from their apartment.

I never met my sister, Donna. My other sister, Linda, was burned nearly to death. I was conceived as the salve on the burns, to fill the abandoned chair at the gray Formica table. My place in the family was cauterized by the flames.

This is the story of my family's trials and triumphs as a result of a tipping of fate. And my own struggle to live up to the role burned into my psyche from the time my mother first dreamed me up as her salvation.

Chapter One
2005

The Rahway River cuts through town, modest houses line its banks, and small yellow and green canoes poke out from wooden docks. The Canoe Club in the center of Cranford rents canoes by the hour for the meandering ride up the river. This river, in this town where my parents raised two daughters, is where we will scatter their ashes.

We lost my father in small bits. His sharp wit, his political opinions, his sarcastic jibes – had been fading with several small strokes. He would forget what he had for breakfast, or that he had to shave–but then he remembered full quotes from Shakespeare. When he hurt his shoulder after a fall, we had no idea it would turn into his final hospital stay. At 90, he went downhill quickly once he was in the hospital and finally congestive heart failure claimed him.

My father's last words to me were "be careful." As far as I know, those were his first to me too. His fear for my safety was one of the only ways he knew to express his love. All through my childhood, and into adulthood, he would read me the newspaper accounts of tragedies befalling people out of the blue.

"Listen to this," he'd start. "This little boy and his mother were walking along Elmora Avenue, probably going to Goodman's Deli, when a piece of scaffolding fell right off a building and killed the kid. Just walking along! You have to be so careful, Judy!"

Or, after I got my driver's license: "This car was just travelling along, minding his own business, when a tractor-trailor cut him off and sent him head first over the rail."

I would nod and tell him I'd be careful. By the time I was an adolescent, I saw it as my sacred duty to prove the world was safer place than my parents believed, that I could take risks and survive.

It made some kind of sense that I was designated as the bad guy to my father in his last years. The one who had to take away his car keys when he was 87 and my mother confided that he would go out and come back hours later after being lost on his way to the grocery store. I was the heavy, too, to decide that they could no longer live by themselves in their apartment. Linda couldn't break away from thinking of my father as her knight, the one who made her feel like she could do anything she set her mind to. I had experienced a different side of my father growing up. His code with me was that I was the daughter who was blessed, that didn't need his praise.

In the hospital days before he died he looked at me, pleading for an answer.

"Why am I going through this? I've been a good man. I would give my right arm for any of my kids. Why is this happening to me?"

I wished then that I had an answer for him that would ease his fears, but he was beyond any of the religious platitudes that gave some people comfort. To him, this was his punishment.

Toward the end, I selfishly wanted to know if I had made him proud in any way.

"So dad," I said to him in one of our last conversations in the hospital. "Am I doing ok–do you think?" I thought I was on safe ground – finally happily married, a good career, a great kid.

A shake of his head, a wrinkle of his brow, pursed lips, a pause, "60-40," he said without looking at me.

That was it–60-40. I knew from my sister that he gave her a much more glowing report just an hour before. She told me that he said he was always very proud of her and what she was able to accomplish, how she raised her daughters. I didn't push it–he was tired–and there were more immediate needs to tend to.

There's an old photo of my father, in his early 40's, in his undershirt, at the kitchen table, holding a cigarette. He never let us see him in his underwear – or even his undershirt. Neither Linda or I could imagine who could have taken such a picture of him.

That modesty is what I thought of when I went back to his hospital room late one night. It was after visiting hours, and I had come back after dinner because I was worried about him. He had called my mother and complained that the pictures on his wall were all moving, and that they were having parties in the hallways. Then the calls had stopped.

Purposefully walking past the security guards, I made my way to his room a little after 10 pm. I found him screaming and writhing naked in his bed. Instinctively, I backed away and ran to get a nurse, sure that he would be mortified to have me find him that way.

It was only seven months after my father died that I found myself in an ambulance with my mother, on our way to a Hospice. The driver's name was Angel.

"Dad would've gotten a kick out of that, the driver being named Angel," I said to my mother over her moans, the noise of the street and the rumble of the vehicle. Trying to calm her, I kept talking. She yelled at each turn with the only means left to her, reaching a new pitch with each bump in the road.

I believed I understood what she was trying to convey to me through her wordless wails:

"What are you doing? Don't move me, I don't need anything anymore, this is not necessary."

Later, Linda insisted I imagined the communication.

"She couldn't have been trying to say anything. She was so far gone by then, and so much morphine."

But I know my mother's voice.

That voice had cut into me a few days back in the hospital when she screamed as they changed her bedding under her. That was the day too that the skin burst from the pressure of fluid gathering at her ankles. It was the first time in years I had seen the real shape of my mother's fabulous legs. And, I was shocked to realize they looked so much like my own.

Now those legs were still. Swaddled in tight sheets to keep her stable on the gurney for the ambulance ride. In fact she was nearly rigid on the narrow bed, only twitching at each bump in the road.

Two days ago she was still lucid and could sit up enough in her hospital bed to take sips of soup and water. Mushroom or tomato soup were all she would eat and so Linda and I took turns harassing the hospital cooks to supply those. We each went down to the basement kitchen and waited until they found the right cans, heated up a bowl and let us take it back up to my mother's room. Between the soup, tracking her meds and trying to make her comfortable, we watched her the way she had always taken care of Linda in the hospital – once a year, every year of her life from the ages of two to twenty when she had surgeries for her injuries from the crash, the skin grafts to be sure she had mobility in her arms and legs, the operation to create a neck where her chin had been burned down into her chest, the failed attempt to reconstruct her ears.

Before and after each of Linda's surgeries, my mother was at her battle station. Flagging nurses for pain medications, dressing changes and bedpans. Asking question after question until she was satisfied with the answers. Why did one skin graft work and another did not? Why wasn't Linda healing at the donor site as quickly as they thought she would? Why was she still in pain?

My mother intuitively knew that specialists were not all equal, and she wanted the best. At least in this, she had some control. When one doctor said they needed to break both of Linda's legs and put her in a body cast for four months to straighten her bowing legs, she and Linda made the rounds to surgeons in several top hospitals, traveling by bus to New York City and Boston to find the right one.

"You're lucky to have us you know," Linda told her while we sat vigil at her bedside.

"You were lucky to have me!" she said, and we laughed because it was true.

On one of the last days we could really communicate with her, I came into her hospital room without my sister. My mother quietly introduced me to her roommate as "my beautiful daughter" – just as Linda re-entered. I instinctively turned to the wall. They exchanged glances, and Linda sat down next to her bed and leaned close to her.

"It's ok Mom, you can call her that."

But she never did again.

In the ambulance, Angel yelled back to me that "we're almost there," before he took a perilously sharp right turn and my mother let out her loudest cry yet.

"Hey can you take it easy up there!" I called up to him, throwing an arm around my mother to quiet her. And, to myself "Is this all I can do to comfort her now? What would she do in my place?"

Even recently, I knew, my mother would talk to Linda about looking into new procedures that might help her. When my sister started having trouble with her hips and knees several years ago in her forties, my mother was just as worried as when Linda was 10. She helped counsel her on what to do, even though Linda is quite medically savvy. My sister still turned to my parents for help and advice when she needed it. They were still all very involved in each other's lives. I was far away from them all.

When we arrived at the Hospice, I felt a calm come over me as the nurses worked to get my mother settled, and were able to quiet her cries. I told the hospice nurse, "She lost a child." That is what she survived, who she was. Somehow it was important that they know.

I pick a secluded spot by the riverbank nestled in trees where we used to feed ducks and have picnics. A small entourage of family is gathered there to meet me.

I hand my father's urn to my cousin to hold and I keep my mother's crooked in my arm like a newborn. We take out the prayer book with notes loosely folded in the front and recite the *Kaddish.*

I look at my Aunt Sylvia and see my father's face. His serious squint, his resolute thin-lipped pout. She is the only one left of his five sisters to say goodbye.

When I had picked up the black box of my mother's remains at the post office, the heavy weight of it overwhelmed me. The brown paper wrapper and postal stamp seemed ludicrous. I carried the package gingerly to my car and cried.

Now, I open up the box to find a plastic bag of ash, closed with a green twist tie. I am a little apprehensive. Will there be chunks of bone? Teeth?

My son Justin takes my father's urn and lifts off the top, releases the plastic bag's twist tie. We lower our packages toward the water and pour both sets of ashes together into the river.

It takes longer than I expected.

"More to us than you knew!" I hear my mother's voice.

The fine gray ash mingles with the brown river water and we watch as the gray cloud is carried downstream.

Chapter Two
BEGINNING THE JOURNEY
2005

I'm sitting on the deck behind my house in a quiet neighborhood in Connecticut, looking out at the pool and the backyard that needs mowing. My husband, David, doesn't want me to mow it anymore since I had trouble with my back a couple of years ago. He'll mow it when he gets home from work, I'll have a couple of cold beers waiting and we can take a swim before we put some steaks on the grill for dinner.

It's a hot day, even in the shade. A couple of years ago there would have been troops of kids splashing and sliding down the slide. Now, though, Justin, is seventeen and his friends come in twos and threes to quietly swim. This new stage of his life has snuck up on me, and I am sometimes surprised by the way he towers over me now and speaks in a deep baritone.

With my cell phone and laptop, I can do some of my freelance writing work outside when the weather is nice – which is what I'm doing today. My parents' deaths had smacked me up against my own mortality and made me take a hard look at my work life. After a 20-year career in corporate communications, I decided I didn't want to play in their game any more. I'm lucky that I've been able to develop a good freelance writing business with some of the same companies I've worked for over the years. So, I have the chance to structure my life differently.

I call my sister, Linda, in Florida. She answers the phone on the first ring.

We talk for a while about our kids, the weather. Then she mentions a new makeup she wants to try that is more natural looking than her last one. I think of the many different brands of makeup she's tried over the years to cover the scars on her face. A red and brown relief map that traces down her neck from just below her eyes. She wears her hair over the remnants of her ears, which she has pierced herself in defiance – no one would do it for her – to wear earrings. Some of the cover-up makeup she's tried has worked well, while others leave her with a whitish mask. I tell her she should try the one she mentions, and then I tell her I want to go back and see the scene of the crime–the crash site.

"Why would you want to do that?" she is incredulous.

I try to explain that since our parents died I've had a nagging feeling that there is something left undone in my own life. It may have something to do with the accident, I say, and going there in the flesh feels suddenly important to me. There have always been missing pieces, for me, in the story. Up until now, I've dismissed the gaps as irrelevant to my life –but now I suspect it is those missing pieces that may hold the seeds of my own truth about my ambivalence toward my father, my historic trouble with men, and my schizophrenic attitude toward risk and safety. I'm hoping the trip back will help me understand more about their lives, and my own.

I remind her that I was never brought back to the scene at Williamson Street, or taken to Donna's grave. My parents never talked about going back to see the spot, and I have no reason to believe that they did. When I get finished explaining my reasons for wanting to visit the crash scene, Linda seems vaguely satisfied with my answer. Nevertheless, she is able to give me specific directions.

"Go up Broad Street toward East Jersey and follow it until you get to South. Take a left and Williamson is a block down, then a right into the old neighborhood."

On the drive, I realize we must have passed this street many times over the years. Certainly when my father had his jewelry store just up the road. But, no one ever acknowledged it to me.

We pass through the lazy suburbs with manicured lawns and two-car garages to the city-like outskirts of Elizabeth. These streets get narrow and are lined with parked cars on both sides. Red brick apartment buildings sprout up between storefronts and three-family houses. Driving down Broad Street I note that it is transformed from what I remember. It used to be a bustling thoroughfare with Buster Brown Shoes, Levy Brother's department store, specialty women's shops and a wide variety of restaurants. Broad street was a destination in those days, when my father's shop was right in the middle of it. Now, people were right when they said it had "gone downhill." Many stores are boarded up, discount stores showcase cheap clothing and junk jewelry. The deli we used to have lunch in next to my father's store is now an Asian grocer.

With each block we pass, layers of my postcard memory are replaced with the raw red meat of a new reality.

We turn off Broad Street onto South and quickly come to the cross street of Williamson. I get out of the car and stand in front of Battin High School, fifty yards from the crash site. Directly across the street is a newish red brick building with clean white striped awnings. It stands at the site of the original yellow brick house where my parents lived with my two sisters.

This is a tiny, precise space. I wonder if the pilot avoided the school purposely, knowing he would save the 300 students inside.

Or, if the story of his signaling his wife by tipping his wing has any truth to it. I think of Linda being carried to this very spot to wait for help.

The local mailman stops to talk. "One of my customers had family killed in that accident, everyone remembers it," he says as he points out the landmarks: a new school, Elizabeth High, across from the old one; the new annex of St. Elizabeth's Hospital down the street.

The place is so different from my suburban childhood home that I cannot envision what my life might have been like here.

But I would not have been here.

Being here is like revisiting the set of an often-played movie – like I have stepped through a looking glass to my family's tale.

At the top of the street, I see for the first time, the exact site of the crash.

This place of an end–and my beginning.

Chapter Three
Out of the Blue

I always knew that my family was formed out of the blue. My version of the stork. Only this stork exchanged a life for a life, had an engine and silver wings.

I learned the details in dribs and drabs – never the whole story. At first I thought it was only a fire that took away my sister, and I wondered for a long time what started the blaze. The word 'accident' was used most often, and I was left to wonder what it meant.

"Before the accident… " I would hear my mother say on the phone, or "…after the accident." It was a way to tell time.

But, somehow, I knew everything they didn't tell me. I felt the pain of my family, without knowing why. A subconscious link informed me of the depth of lingering grief, bitterness and anger. I intuited the pain they felt in watching Linda go through so much physical and psychological turmoil. I understood their investment in me, but also my father's hesitance.

My sister Linda was hurt, I knew that because she went into the hospital every year to get something fixed, or "reconstructed." But, she didn't look different to me. In fact, I only noticed her scars when others reacted to them.

The first time I remember understanding she was different was at Goodman's Deli when I was six or seven. We'd go there with my father for hot pastrami on rye with a little mustard for me, corned beef on rye for Linda. Egg creams and fries, of course. When we sat down, I noticed a little boy in the booth across the aisle staring at Linda. I watched as she tried not to pay attention, but I saw her glance at him, then look back down at her menu. I knew only that I wanted to protect her from that boy before his hurtful words could leave even more scars. I stared him down until he dropped his gaze.

After that, I tried to force myself to look at Linda with new eyes. To see what others saw. It wasn't easy to do. I didn't know her any other way. But, I made myself study the worst scars. Most of the bottom half of her face down her neck had raised red scar tissue. Both of her ears were gone, though her hearing was fine. Her left arm and leg were badly burned, wrapped tight in tough, brownish red where the skin had burned down to muscle. Before she started wearing makeup as a teenager, the scars on her face drew attention away from her wide, green Bette Davis eyes, which were in fact beautiful. The flames had seared the skin under her cheekbone, collared her neck and descended down her chest.

At some point, as I got older, I started listening more carefully to snippets of conversations to grasp the entirety of the story of "the accident." The extended family always talked like the details were well known and there was no need to bring up something that was so painful. And certainly never to mention Donna's name. My father, especially, never uttered her name.

Except that I wasn't there. Even when there was some talk about it, it would stop when I walked in the room. It felt like a conspiracy to keep me separate. Something told me that I should not ask questions. I might break the spell and disappear.

I remember being stunned when I first heard it had been an airplane that had crashed and burned in my mother's kitchen. I'm sure she was telling the story to a new friend on the phone when

I overheard her. When I asked her about it, she seemed just as surprised that I didn't already know.

"You know about the accident, Judy, right? The plane crash? Your sister is burned..."

Like it all was as plain as the nose on my face.

And then, hearing my mother tell about her pregnancies, the way that women tell their horror stories about birth, I was shocked to hear there were three.

"All three of my babies were big," she'd say. "My first was over 10 lbs! But, she came easily. Linda was another story–she had a hard time. She didn't want to be born. They had to dislocate her shoulders to get her out."

My parents must have had some kind of unspoken agreement not to dwell on the accident. Maybe when I was born, they developed this pact to put it all behind them and go on with this new life. Just another reconstructive surgery.

Then there were the stories told time and again, meant to bring me into the family drama, since I came in during ACT II. But, mostly, they reinforced the central focus of the family–my sister.

There was the bus story. The doctor told my parents that they needed to get Linda out in public soon after the accident, to get used to the reactions she may get from people and to learn how to deal with them.

The plan was to take a city bus from the apartment to downtown Elizabeth, walk the few blocks to my father's jewelry store and all go out for lunch. It was Linda's first pubic exposure since the crash. But on the way, she fell on some loose stones and split open the fragile scar tissue on her knee. Just then the bus pulled up. They took seats near the bus driver and my mother pulled some tissues from her purse to dab at the bloodied knee, when she noticed a woman staring intently at Linda.

"What happened to her–what did you do to her?"

My mother took a moment to pull herself together, and think about what to say.

"But, I really couldn't help myself," she said when she told the story. "I turned to her and said, 'She was in an accident. An airplane crashed into my house and killed my other daughter–and my baby here is lucky to be alive. Do you have any more questions I can answer for you right now?' That woman didn't have a thing to say for the rest of that ride!"

My father told about taking Linda to her first Thanksgiving Day parade. I was just six months old, at home while my mother cooked dinner. He told Linda she would see the Shriners in their little hats, in their tiny cars whizzing around. He prepared her for the loud sirens and music, so that she wouldn't be afraid.

At the parade, shiny new fire trucks showed off their bells and sirens, clanging in time with the tubas in the high school band. Local royalty rode in convertibles waving and throwing wrapped candy to the children that lined the streets. The Boy and Girl Scouts were flanked by the Little League and Daughters of the American Revolution.

They found a spot in front of Levy Brothers department store, out of the wind and cold, to watch the parade. My father bought a red balloon from a street vendor and Linda was happily clutching it when a little boy approached her, pointed into her smiling face and squealed, "Eeew–what happened to you?"

Linda burst into tears. The boy's mother dragged him away with a shake of her head. My father scooped Linda up quickly to hug her, trying to control her sobs.

"Honey, don't ever forget that some people are pretty on the outside, and ugly on the inside. You are just wearing your badge of courage on the outside, and you should always wear it with pride."

These were the kinds of stories that filled in the gaps for me as a child. That gave me the definition of what our family was about. I was not a lead actor in this play.

When I wanted to go on a trip to Florida with my friends in high school, I learned more about the actual crash. Our family did not fly. My parents had only recently taken their first airplane ride on a business trip, and Linda had never flown. To boot, my flight was scheduled on American Airlines–the very carrier that crashed a plane into their home. I was 16 years old, and totally oblivious to the ramifications of their putting me on that particular plane by myself. They gritted their teeth and let me go.

Chapter Four
JANUARY 22, 1952
Day of the Crash
7:00 AM

My mother woke up early, as usual, to get my father off to work, her seven-year-old off to school, and breakfast for her mother and two-year-old Linda.

They lived on the second floor of a three-story brick building which resembled a stack of washed out, yellowed Lego blocks. It also housed another family and one boarder on the third floor. A candy store on the ground level was a gathering place for local teenagers.

Sounds filtered up from the store and down from the family upstairs having their breakfast as they got ready for the day. My mother was held hostage in the middle.

She had planned their day around Linda's doctor appointment later that morning. A spunky young mother, she had energy to spare. Her hair was always expertly coiffed by her own hand, clothes neatly pressed for both she and her two girls. My mother was the kind to strike up a conversation in the checkout line at the grocery store and to show up with a bundt cake at a new neighbor's door. Her family was her core.

My father was a generally happy man with thinning black hair and an unwavering smile. He reveled in his young family. My mother took it in stride that he was reserved in showing affection. She had decided she could make up for it by showing him how.

Two years older than my mother, my father had held a plethora of jobs during the depression years. Sometimes two or three at a time. First, struggling to help his parents feed his five sisters–and now for his own girls. He painted houses with his father, delivered laundry, was a milkman, worked in a pharmacy–and now worked in a jewelry store.

This morning my father wanted only his usual toast and coffee.

"Some eggs or some oatmeal maybe Al? You can't work for hours on a piece of toast." My mother worried that he didn't eat right when he was away from her. He was thin as a rail, and she suspected he only made time for coffee and cigarette breaks during the day.

After 15 years of marriage, she still thought she could change his habits.

"Nope, that's all I need. And hugs from my girls, of course," he said.

He reached over to give little Linda a tender squeeze. Donna, the seven-year-old, came over to his chair for a full-on goodbye hug, wrapping her arms around his neck and holding her cheek next to his for a moment. A warm knot took hold of his chest as he hugged her back.

"Bye daddy, have a good day," she told him.

He let her hang on for a minute, then extracted himself.

My mother pecked him on the cheek, handed him his coat and his black "Dick Tracy" hat and he was out the door. Whistling, he sprang into his 1950 Buick SPECIAL with the black leather seats. He loved getting into that car–the first car he ever owned–and driving the couple of miles to his job at Goldblatt Jewelers. He lit a cigarette from the car lighter; inhaling his first puff deeply, opened the front side-vent window and slowly began to drive away.

Donna waved from the window.

Chapter Five
1953

After the surgery to lift Linda's chin off of her chest where flames had welded the two together, she needed X-ray treatments to prevent keloid (thickened) scars from forming. She was three and a half.

My mother said that when Linda saw the gigantic X-ray machine, she became hysterical and could not be calmed.

As the technicians tried to restrain her, my mother intervened, quickly grabbing Linda up from the table and ordering them to stop. They just shook their heads–their schedule blown for the morning.

"There's no reason to put her through this now. I'll bring her back in a week," my mother told them. "She'll be ready then. Give me a week." And, she ushered Linda from the exam room.

At home, my parents built a mini-model of the X-ray machine–just the size for Linda's doll, Sandy, to use. My father was diligent in constructing the X-ray machine model, finding pictures in the library of the actual machine used in the hospital and replicating it with tin foil and cardboard.

For a week, Linda gave Sandy her X-ray treatments every day, positioning her carefully and lowering the model X-ray machine close to her, but never touching her. My mother explained exactly what would happen to Sandy each time:

"She just has to lie still while the machine does its job, and she won't feel anything, see honey?"

It was a brilliant ploy, putting Linda in charge and showing her that Sandy was unharmed.

Sandy had black hair and green eyes just like Linda. When Linda went into surgery, Sandy did too. Operating Room nurses always made sure that Sandy had the exact same bandages as Linda. And, they used the doll to explain what would happen to her before each surgery.

Chapter Six
2005

My coffee is getting cold on my desk. There is work for me to get at, but I can't seem to concentrate on the brochure draft I'm meant to deliver tomorrow to a client. This new insurance product is not holding my interest. I'm searching for new words to say 'best' that their legal team will let me use. *Improved… competitive… enhanced…*

Instead of working, I wind up heating up my coffee in the microwave and bringing it downstairs to the basement where I've stored my parents' things; the photo albums and memorabilia that I brought back with me from their apartment.

Years ago, when I first told them I wanted to write, they began giving me clips from the newspaper accounts of the crash. They started writing down notes for me. Then, Linda joined in to add her stories. At the time, I took a look at it all and shoved it into a file folder without much thought. Now their notes are a gift that helps me pull the story together and see my place in it.

A ragged manila folder holds my mother's longhand on several yellow legal pads with her many attempts to put the story down on paper. On paper, she had relived it again and again, using different verbs and adjectives, but always ending up with one daughter gone, one daughter brought back from the dead.

In the same folder is an envelope with yellowed newspaper clippings that chronicle the event and offer journalistic snapshots: The day of the accident; hospital treatment; the funeral; the investigation.

Reading the news stories, I recognize the familiar feeling of being separate from my family, like I have always been pressing my nose up against the glass trying to get inside.

The clips only graze the surface of the story I want to know. Even the notes left by my family tell me only snippets. How did my parents survive losing their first-born child and watching their other baby go through the agony of being burned over 80% of her body and the resulting medical care? How were they able to maintain their marriage through it all? And, what was my part? How did they have the courage to even have me?

Whenever I have a new project, whether it's writing a marketing piece, a news article or a feature story, I first immerse myself in the facts surrounding the topic. It's a technique I've used since my early days as a reporter, in hopes that the story will bubble up from the minutest detail.

This trail is old, 50 years plus, but Elizabeth fireman Gary Haszko remembers it when I call the fire department. He wasn't there, but he digs in the archives and sends me news clips and an 8"x10" photo of the apartment building just after the crash.

I have never seen this photo before. It didn't show up in any of the newspapers so far. The detail in it mesmerizes me. It shows smoke still spewing from the building, firemen standing in the front door pointing a hose up the splintered stairwell. It looks like the picture was taken just after they quelled the flames, and I imagine what was going inside at this moment. I conjure Donna in the scene, lying in a pile of smoldering ash, trapped under a blackened beam, fighting for her life. I try to see her face, but my mind's eye

only registers a small lifeless body, nearly indistinguishable from the black ash surrounding her.

I picture firefighters sifting through the rubble, spotting her remains camouflaged in the scorched splinters, and I no longer wonder why it took nearly 12 hours to find her.

I get out a magnifying glass to search the faces, to stare at the second story window and look for my sister.

Chapter Seven
JANUARY 22, 1952
DAY OF THE CRASH
7:30 AM

Dad, Mom, Donna, Linda

"Ok girls, let's get going," my mother clapped her hands for attention.

"Donna, are you getting dressed? Linda, come on over here, honey, and let's finish our breakfast. You can see Donna later when she gets home. Mom! We're going out soon. Your breakfast is on the table. We'll be back a little after noon."

Finished with breakfast, the three headed out to walk Donna to school. Donna was pretty and petite with clear green eyes. She had on her black jumper with a white blouse underneath, the lace of the collar tickling the edge of her cheek. The night before, my mother curled her chestnut brown hair into a pageboy. Now, she furrowed her brow at her mother.

"I don't need those leggings Mom, I'm too old for them!"

Her little girl was growing up so fast, she thought. "At least put your gloves on!"

Linda was content to be snuggled up warmly in full winter garb, protected from head to toe with wool leggings, sweater, coat, hat and mittens. My mother threw her coat over herself and buttoned it on the way out the door, grabbing both girls' hands for the short walk to Woodrow Wilson School 19.

There was a light mist falling, and in the dense fog my mother could not see around the next corner.

Chapter Eight 1952 TO 1957

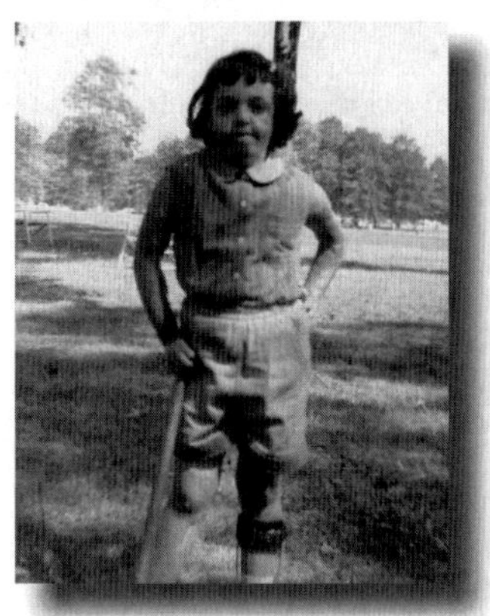

For most of 1952, my parents lived in a hotel while Linda stayed in the hospital. Late in the year, they were able to move to the Warnanco Village Apartments in Elizabeth that we called "The Village." When she was well enough, Linda came home to the new apartment and my mother got busy lining up friends for her among her new neighbors. She managed to find all the mothers with girls around Linda's age and recruited them to her cause. As a result, Linda had a group of loyal friends she felt safe with and camaraderie she cherished for a very long time.

One day, the boys included the girls in their after-school baseball game–mainly because they didn't have enough players–in the courtyard behind the apartment complex.

The captains took turns picking girls for their teams, until Linda was left standing alone. At the time, Linda wore a brace on her left leg up to her knee with a shoe like a man's work boot.

Linda ran home, as best she could, and cried to her mother, "They don't want to play with me."

My mother was hesitant to intervene with explanations and her usual plea for understanding. She knew Linda should start taking over this role for herself.

Just as she considered what to do, she heard a commotion outside. Out the window, she and Linda saw an animated argument between the boys and girls. Hands on hips, fingers pointing, girls shouting, boys cowering. Within minutes, her friend Nancy Boroff knocked on the door, marched in and pulled Linda's arm to go back outside.

"We told those boys we aren't playing unless you play. JoAnn, Janie, Sue and me, we all told 'em," Nancy told Linda proudly. With a grateful lump in her throat, Linda joined the game.

Nancy was a skinny, high energy little girl with wide eyes and ash blonde curls. Later on, I loved her because she always brought me a present when she visited. But her best gift was the friendship she lavished on my big sister.

Together, they had contests to see who could jump over the hedges from a moving swing. They would roller skate through clotheslines of clean clothes, chased by the women who had just hung them out. They had wars with wagons full of berries they picked from the bushes behind the apartments. They made costumes and put on talent shows for their parents.

Linda felt so normal with her friends that she sometimes forgot her limitations.

"Let's go play by the brook in the woods," Nancy suggested one day after school. A small gathering of trees behind the apartments passed for woods. The shallow brook could be crossed by hopping from rock to rock as stepping stones, requiring a full leap between them.

Linda had been warned that she shouldn't go near water, that it would ruin her brace and shoe. But when Nancy hopped from one rock to the next, she followed despite her heavy metal brace.

Pretty soon, she lost her footing and fell in. The brace and orthopedic shoe were soaked, ruined.

Linda panicked, "My mother is going to kill me! I can't get this wet. She's warned me a zillion times!"

"Don't worry, I'll tell her. I'll take the blame," Nancy said. "It's my fault anyways, I shouldn't have brought you here."

They slogged back to the apartment, the waterlogged shoe and brace weighing Linda down. They stood on the front stoop for several long minutes and just as Nancy got the courage to knock on the door–it opened.

My mother saw Linda dripping wet and ushered them both inside.

She yelled, "Oh, my God, how could you?" Her Hungarian temper flaring, knowing how upset my father would be about the expensive shoe and brace. But she couldn't bring herself to really be mad.

Secretly, she thought, "This is what normal kids do."

Chapter Nine
A Recurring Scene

I was five. I was six. I was seven. I was eight.

I sat on the edge of Linda's bed with her little brown and tan plaid suitcase open next to me, watching her pack slippers, underwear and nightgowns.

"Don't worry, Jude," Linda said. "I'll be back before you know it. And stay away from my stuff, will ya?"

Instead of an answer, I started picking apart one of the raised balls of fabric on her white chenille bedspread.

"Hey, cut that out –you'll ruin it!"

I wanted her to yell at me. That just felt more normal. Better than thinking about her going into the hospital again, and about what they would do to her there. There was never much explanation to me about what would happen to her, and so my mind was left to wander about the cutting, moving bones and skin and re-attaching pieces of her like some giant jigsaw puzzle. I tried to imagine it all without any blood, like in the movies when they cut away from the surgery scene and you only see the patient later recovering in bed. All pristine and clean and neat without even a drop of blood at the site of the intravenous needle. But, when I closed my eyes I saw the blood, remembered the raw skin graft sites I saw when her bandages were changed, the reddened stitches and bloody gauze pads. I felt lucky and guilty about it at the same time, that I didn't have to be cut with scalpels and prodded with needles. That I could stay safely behind.

Some of the surgeries were to replace scarred skin with better skin from another part of Linda's body, so she would have two places she would be healing. One where scar tissue was removed and replaced, and the other at the donor site where healthy tissue was taken from. She had one surgery to try to reconstruct her burned ears, but the donor ears were rejected and had to be taken off.

When Linda went in for surgery, my mother always went away, too. She'd be in the hospital in New York with Linda when she had the operation, and then stay in her room for the first few nights. After that she might come back at night, and go right back in the morning until Linda came home. Every year it was a couple of months before it was over.

It was very lonely at home without them. Very quiet. My father read the paper when he got home from work and we would heat up a dinner that my mother left for us. I'd watch the news with him, he'd ask how school was, and did I do my homework.

I was happy to have my father all to myself then, but not without a stab of guilt, feeling that my happiness must mean that I was glad Linda was in the hospital.

On Saturdays my father brought me to his jewelry store to help out. When I was too little to wait on customers, I helped wrap gifts and polish up rings in the back. When a gift wrap was needed he'd call me out to the front counter and introduce me to the customer with his arm around me. He'd give me instructions about what kind of gift it was and which paper to use. It felt like we were a team. My pay was sometimes a piece of jewelry; a ruby ring or a new charm for my bracelet.

At night, I would stand next to my father to hear as my mother talked. Snippets would filter through to me from their conversation:

"Why did Linda have a bad reaction to the anesthesia? Was it different?"

"Well, how long did they say it would be before she healed from this?"

"What do you mean they don't know if it's going to take."

Mostly, I didn't know what any of it meant. But I could tell from his voice, the crease in my father's forehead, or if he sat down heavily on the kitchen chair next to the phone as he listened to the report from my mother.

After about a week I could usually go up to see her. I liked to bring her candy or a magazine. Even when she was all bandaged up, with tubes coming out of her, or casts on her legs, she always greeted me with "Hey, Jude!" when I came in.

Visiting Linda with both of my parents felt like the whole family was together again. We would hang around all day, even after visiting hours were over. My father always told some joke that got her laughing. Sometimes she'd even have to tell him to stop. My mother would give him "the look" and he'd settle down. Most often, though, he'd make her laugh again at least once before we left. He always left her with a laugh, but when we left he'd be like a deflated balloon. When my mother stayed behind in NY and he and I would go home alone, it was always a silent ride.

When I was in second grade, I had eye surgery to correct my crossed eyes. I remember expecting the same level of drama that surrounded Linda whenever she went to the hospital.

But when I packed my pajamas, slippers and Tiny Tears doll in Linda's usual hospital suitcase, no one acted like it was much of a big deal. It was like I was going to a sleepover party.

Linda looked a little worried when I left with my parents. She hugged me and said, "Don't worry Jude, you'll be home before you know it!" That made me feel better, and I tried to make myself remember to say that to her next time she was leaving.

The hospital in New York City was gigantic inside and even though I was holding my mother's hand, I felt lost.

Everything was white metal and glass. The ceiling was so high I had to put my head all the way back to see it. People were moving everywhere around me, but I couldn't hear them. They were silent walkers in white and green. I shivered with goose bumps.

The doctor explained something about putting me to sleep for the operation, with "magic gas" so he could fix my eyes with tiny tools. I pictured him tying knots in the muscles in my eyes to make them tighter, pulling the eyeballs to the center.

We went up to the fourth floor, into a long hallway full of beds. I counted fifteen before we got to mine.

A nurse pulled a curtain all the way around my bed and I changed into the hospital nightgown. It was very thin and I shivered more.

I had expected that my mother would stay with me at the hospital, like she always did with Linda, but on the elevator my father talked about how they were going home and would be leaving soon.

"We'll be here when you have the surgery tomorrow kiddo," he said. He smiled and squeezed my shoulder, but I was having none of it and shook him off.

My mother put a shopping bag next to my bed with the books she brought for me. She went to a sink down the hall and filled a water pitcher, put it on my nightstand next to a plastic cup, fluffed the pillows behind my back and tucked Tiny Tears in next to me. She looked like she wanted to stay, but my father took her hand and they gave me a hug and left.

I couldn't catch my breath and my eyes filled up when I watched them walk away down the hall. I thought about how Linda did this all the time and tried to be a "good little soldier" like her. But there was no one to see me do it, so I just curled up with Tiny Tears.

Chapter Ten
2005

This afternoon is quiet at home. Justin is still at school and David won't be home from work for a few more hours. The energy in the house is different when I'm alone here. David is my comrade and confidant. We talk through dinners about our day, what's on our minds, our schedules, the news we heard. Even though we've been married a short time, we seem to have a shared past. Maybe because we are nearly the exact same age, or grew up in similar suburban New Jersey towns and come from Jewish backgrounds. Whatever the reason, we have felt like old souls from the beginning of our relationship. I can count on his steadiness in any situation and I am spoiled by a man who puts my feelings and happiness ahead of his own. At times, I think he is too good for me.

David and I were early adopters of online dating in 1997. He was just coming out of a divorce and was struggling to make a new life for himself, while still being there for his three sons. I had been divorced for nearly seven years. We joke that it was kismet that we both bought computers the same week and happened to try out a new dating site. Neither one of us was into the bar scene to meet people. It was even more amusing that he lived about five minutes from me. We both shopped at the same Stop & Shop supermarket around the corner.

I had been on three disastrous dates over the past couple of weeks with men I met on the site when David and I struck up a conversation online. His emails were sincere and funny, so I decided to meet him. I dropped Justin off at my friend's house and told her, "This is absolutely the last date I'm going on."

We planned to meet at a local restaurant and when I saw David waiting outside for me I was relieved that it seemed he had been truthful in his online profile. He had a full head of dark hair, a kind, handsome face, and looked fit in his red sweater. At dinner, David seemed a little nervous and it took awhile for him to start talking. I thought it was cute that he was sort of shy. We exchanged the first date preliminaries, much like a job interview. Where we worked, details of our kids, status of our relationships with our ex-spouses. When he talked about his sons, I could see how devoted he was to them, and to doing the best for them, which further endeared him to me. We agreed that divorce was a complicated thing for adults, and even more confusing for the kids who have no vote in the outcome.

After dinner, we made the evening last a little longer by taking a walk and talking more. We weren't running out of conversation – a very good sign I thought. By the end of the evening, we had been laughing quite a lot.

After three failed marriages, I was being very careful who I got involved with, so at the end of this evening I held out my hand to shake his. David looked hurt and asked if he could kiss me goodnight. That tickled me to be asked, and we kissed in the parking lot quickly. It was enough, though, to recognize a spark of passion between us.

I tried to stay objective as we got more seriously involved, remembering my earlier therapy sessions that pointed to my propensity to throw out reason when I fell for someone. I looked up my self-help books and the notes I made about why I had chosen the wrong mates in the past.

I told myself I didn't want to get married again since I was so bad at it. My primary responsibility, I felt, was raising my son well. I remember David and I having conversations early on that neither of us was looking for a long-term relationship. He was so newly divorced and still in the throws of adjusting. In fact, we didn't even meet each other's children for quite awhile. We dated on the off weekends when our ex-spouses had the kids, negotiating our schedules so they coincided. Then, of course, it all changed when we fell in love.

I had made long lists of the traits of my three past husbands and corresponded elements of my childhood to my choices. It had been an awakening for me to recognize the similarities in the three men that I had thought were so different. They were all very critical of me, something I didn't see myself until friends pointed it out, for everything from what I wore to my cooking. They all shared an insecurity that manifested in putting me down in some way. Each one was emotionally distant, not wanting to talk about feelings or issues between us. All but one had trouble showing affection.

By the time I met David, I was prepared to put all that self-work to good use. It was a lot to track in a new relationship. I mentally went through my checklist as the relationship evolved, and it was passing all the preliminary screening. We talked openly about how we felt about our past. David was accessible and honest. He was the most stable person I had ever been involved with and had been at the same insurance company for twenty years when we met. And, although he was shy at first, once he opened up, he made me laugh more than anyone I had ever known and we had an immediately strong connection.

Now, Justin fills the house with the exuberance of a teenage boy. His friends are in and out, his music sometimes too loud, his clothes and belongings scattered around the place. And, even when I complain about some of it – I have to admit I love it. All the ragged edges of his growing up, and even the small annoyances make it real, and make me part of his life

I can't believe that this is his senior year in high school, and that next year he will be off to college. It doesn't seem possible that time has passed so quickly. This fall, we took a few trips to visit schools in Upstate New York, Boston and Amherst, Massachusetts. The trips together reminded me of how it was when it was just he and I, after the divorce from his father, my third husband. We were quite a team when it was just us, for six years, before I married David (my fourth husband if you are keeping track). Justin and I took lots of road trips back then, to visit friends in Pennsylvania, family in Washington and in Florida. By the age of six, he was a practiced travelling companion happily seated either beside me or in back, depending on his size at the time, singing along with me to *Truckin'* or *Friend of the Devil.* He learned how to use maps to help me navigate, and was patient when I got lost. Now he's applying to schools and writing essays. I'm mostly writing checks.

I take a notebook and pen down to the family room to continue my research for the book I have decided I want to write. My parents' notes to me have an urgency now, almost insisting that I pay attention, that I try to tell the story. I'm still wondering whose story it will be: theirs or mine.

I have three storage boxes full of writings, clippings and photographs to go through. There's also a musty leather suitcase chock full of my parents' things. Sitting in the middle of the floor, I surround myself with the loot and start looking through it. Today's mission, I decide, is to find out something about my parents' lives that I didn't know.

My parents seemed to have sprung to life at the time of their meeting. Before that time, their individual histories are sketchy for me. Partially, that may be because the fire took away any photos of them as children. I don't recall seeing even one of either of them before they were together.

My mother and father were introduced by my mother's brother, Arty. He and my father were best friends in high school. My father was 16 when the Depression hit hard and he left school to take a job to help his family, but he and Arty remained friends. Arty had a little sister, Florence (my mother), and when she turned 18 my father noticed more and more that she had blossomed into a lovely young woman.

My father told me the story of how he asked Arty to introduce him to his sister time and time again, but Arty refused, telling him he was not her type. My father didn't give up.

"I have two steady jobs, I'm industrious, I'm supporting my family for God sakes. And let's face it, I'm adorable," he told him, until one day, he talked Arty into inviting him for dinner.

It was a gray, rainy Friday evening in April. The few cars on the road, bulbous and glistening, crackled through the slick streets, kicking up spray from their white-wall tires. The town bustled with people walking home from work and school. On Friday night in a Jewish neighborhood, most everyone rushed home to make dinner for Shabbat at sunset.

My father wore his best clothes– clean white shirt, dark tie, pressed black dress pants, spit-shined shoes. He walked in to the small brick building, and up the two flights to the apartment that housed Arty's family: his mother Hermina; his father Desher (David in English); brothers Henry and Eddie; and his beautiful sister, Florence.

Before ringing the bell, my father took a moment to collect himself. When the door opened, my father swaggered in with a quick smile, but backed up two steps when he took in the three brothers flanking my mother. With dark soft curls and wide expressive green eyes, my mother was the family jewel.

Nodding to them, he offered his hand to her, which Eddie intercepted.

"Very nice to meet you. I'm Al Mandel," he said, shaking Eddie's hand, moving on to Henry, and finally my mother, who averted her eyes.

Before dinner my mother lit the Sabbath candles, saying the blessing by heart. Wearing a shawl over her head, she waved the heat of the flames upward toward her face. Her mother and father looked on with pride, keeping their eye on my father, who couldn't keep his eyes off my mother.

The cacophony of conversation was a mix of English, Yiddish and Hungarian. My father tried to answer the parents' Hungarian questions in Yiddish, and to keep up with the brothers' banter in English. My mother took pity on him and began to translate. Soon, they had made up a blend of English, Yiddish and Hungarian that got them laughing, and the brothers staring suspiciously.

I know this hybrid language well. They spoke it all through my childhood when they didn't want my sister and I to understand.

At dinner, my father fit in a few jokes, in both Yiddish and English, careful to keep them clean. He got some laughs, but Papa Desher remained stone-faced.

Dinner was a traditional Sabbath meal, with a freshly killed chicken from the neighborhood kosher butcher, roasted potatoes, green beans and Hermina's home-baked challah bread. Nearly the same exact meal was now being served at my father's own house. In fact, he went to the butcher that afternoon for his mother.

He hated watching the slaughter. The chicken's neck stretched across the chopping block to be severed quickly and completely, causing the least amount of suffering possible, according to Jewish law. Then the chicken, still moving without its head, sometimes actually running, for a moment before it drops. The carcass hung upside down to let the blood drain out into a pan placed below the open cut of the neck. My father always looked away.

When they finished dinner, my father gave Arty a serious look and flicked his head toward the front door. Outside, they sat down on the stoop to talk and smoke.

"Well, what do I do now?" he asked his friend. "Can I ask her out now? Is it ok?"

"You'll have to talk to my father first, then you can ask her."

Desher had retired to his easy chair with his pipe. He was stoking it when my father walked in. Somehow, the right words came out, and Desher gave a nod of his head, a wave of his hand.

"Go back out on the front stoop and I'll send Florence out," Arty instructed.

In a few minutes my mother appeared. She smoothed the apron that covered her Sabbath dress, looking down at her sensible black shoes. My father offered his hand to help her sit beside him on the step.

"I like your family," he said, grinning.

My mother rolled her eyes, took his hand, "They're not easy, that's for sure. But they're mine and they mean well for me."

"I know, I can see that. That's why I like them so much."

They sat and talked about movies, about the new singer they just heard, Frank Sinatra– until they heard…

"Flurrrrennnce….in!" Desher, standing at the front door, yelled in his thick Hungarian accent.

In their wedding photo three years later, my father stands tall in his tailed tux, looking proud to have snagged this beauty. My mother is in her white Belgian lace dress with the 40 buttons up the front. Her flowers are drooping slightly in the 100-degree heat of August 8th, 1937.

Chapter Eleven
JANUARY 22, 1952
DAY OF THE CRASH
7:40 AM

A few blocks away from my family's home, at 611 Broad Street, Captain Thomas John Reid was getting ready to pilot American Airlines commuter flight #6780 from Newark to Rochester, Syracuse and Buffalo and back again that evening.

Just a month before, Captain Reid flew to Japan for American Airlines on a mission to return Korean combat veterans. A plane on a similar mission crashed in British Columbia, killing 36 people. He tricked fate once.

He was experienced, with 7,062 hours of piloting, and the fog and frost of the day didn't pose a problem for him on this short flight. Maybe he was thinking about his new baby that was on the way, or his mother-in-law's birthday party that night.

Chapter Twelve
Donna & Me

Donna was an only child for five years before Linda came along. She was the nucleus of the small family, the sun around which all revolved.

After the crash, a scrapbook of letters written by all of her second grade classmates was given to my parents as a tribute. Letters like "Dear Donna, I know you are up in heaven now. We will miss you, but we know you are happy." Or, "Dear Donna, I hope they have your favorite vanilla cupcakes in heaven."

We had at least one thing in common: we both loved picnics in the park with my mother. My mother had a way of making an ordinary outing into an event, so I know how Donna felt when they spread out a quilted blanket on the expansive green lawn and unpacked her favorite snacks. I bet my mother invented her grape cone for Donna before me. That was when she would spiral aluminum foil into a cone around her fist, and then fill it to overflowing with green or red grapes. She made the bottom into a handle of sorts, so I could carry it around and play while I ate the grapes. I was a fidgety child who couldn't sit still for very long, which was another reason for the grape cone, but it doesn't seem likely that Donna and I shared that restless trait. The image I was always given of Donna was of a perfect, calm and obedient girl.

My mother would bring a grape cone with her whenever she got a call from school that I was sick. I always felt calm as soon as she came into the school nurse's office.

"She's not feeling well, again, Mrs. Mandel," the nurse would say.

I wouldn't look at the nurse, who suspected me of faking. She interrogated me every time I got sent into her office, at least once a week when I felt sick to my stomach and on the verge of throwing up.

My mother didn't ask questions. "Let's go honey," she'd say. "We'll go visit the ducks."

I'd get up silently and take her hand, avoiding the nurse's gaze. My mother's blue Dodge Dart was parked right in front of school and I hopped in the front seat. This already made it a special day since I usually had to sit in the back.

We'd drive down Springfield Avenue until we got to the center of town. At the bridge, we turned left, passed the white gazebo, and drove along the riverbank until we got to our special spot with the park bench. By that time my stomach had settled down and the nausea had subsided.

The ducks sensed our arrival and clustered at the river's edge. They scrambled for the few pieces of bread I'd throw into the river.

My mother would be beside me, bundled in her brown quilted car coat with the fur collar. Her oversized pocketbook was filled with bread for the ducks and snacks for me.

There'd be a sandwich with two slices of bologna, on white bread cut in quarters, with just a touch of mustard. The grape cone would come out when she saw I couldn't sit still any longer. Then sometimes a package of Twinkies to share.

"Nerves" our family doctor said about my constant stomachaches.

"What kind of nerves can an 8-year-old have?!" my father said.

The doctors in New York City didn't know either. They made me drink chalky white liquid and wait hours for it to run through me in order to take x-rays. Or they'd pump me full of the stuff from the other end.

My parents were convinced that my stomach problems were caused by my worry over Linda. There was some truth that my illness coincided with her hospitalizations. My mother always pointed to the comment on my kindergarten report card that "Judy carries the world on her shoulders."

Or maybe I just wanted to feed the ducks with my mother–have her all to myself for a change, sit in the front seat and have my own grape cone. And every once in awhile, have my mother put her arm around me and give me a squeeze.

Other than our love of picnics, and my mother, it didn't appear to me that Donna and I were anything alike. The portrait I was given of Donna was painted with small, deliberate strokes. Her image took shape through layers of stories, sideways glances, and quivering sighs. I was told that when Linda was born, Donna felt the baby was brought home from the hospital just for her. She took my mother's lead and held Linda with loving care, begging to feed and diaper her. My mother said it was Donna's nature to envelope her new baby sister in her love, and to instinctively know that her parents had enough love to give to both their girls. There was never a moment's jealousy, according to my mother. Linda was her new playmate, her cherished baby doll.

On a day not long before the crash, she asked my parents if she could bring home a new friend for dinner one night. They agreed and when the evening arrived, my mother said she was shocked.

"She never mentioned that her new friend was a Negro girl. That just wasn't done back then."

My father might have used a different word, and was probably much more alarmed. But it was their first sign that their daughter might be there to teach them something.

People called Donna "ahead of her time" or "too good for this world." But maybe she would have changed it.

"She was such a special child," my mother said. "She had a kindness within her, a quality that made everyone want to be near her." Donna was their "little angel." The comparison between us was unspoken, but always present. My father would admonish my mother for spoiling me, catering to my selfish nature, for example, by buying me a balloon at the checkout counter at the grocery store, or the new toy I saw on TV.

The angel legacy was reinforced by actual documentation. Eleanor C. Delaney, the principal of Woodrow Wilson School 19, where Donna had attended second grade, wrote a condolence letter to my parents, published in the *Elizabeth Daily Journal:*

"Donna will always be, to you and to all of us who loved her, the Donna of yesterday – sweet, lovely, unspoiled. She will always be, to all of us, a child we love who will be forever fresh and young and innocent.

"Her outstanding native ability could have made her disliked by children who had less ability, except that her sweetness, unselfishness and genuine consideration for others prevented her from ever wanting to monopolize the scene–as she could have done so easily. It was your influence which kept her unspoiled in spite of her unusual native gifts of attractiveness, intelligence and everything it takes to make a wonderful girl."

I could imagine my parents' disappointment at having that angel replaced with a mere mortal. When I was a toddler our family would get together with my Aunt Maxine's family often. The adults would sit around the dining room table and talk for hours while they sipped coffee and nibbled on cheese or prune Danish. My mother would get out her matching coffee cups and dessert plates, and be sure the percolator was full. Linda would sit at the table and listen to the re-told family stories. My cousin, Henry, and I were close in age, and we would play with Tinker Toys or Lincoln Logs in the living room, in view of our parents. My Aunt Maxine told me they would watch me play and compare me with Donna. Did I share the same way? Did I play as intelligently, or show the same empathy that she would have?

"She's not like Donna," my father would say. "Donna was something very special."

"But she's a sweet girl," my aunt told me she would defend me.

I'm not sure my father ever forgave me for being here when Donna was not.

The only time I remember my father ever speaking of Donna was when we talked about planning his own funeral. He was in his eighties then, nearly fifty years after Donna's death. We were sitting out on the porch at their condo in Florida. He was playing solitaire with the deck of cards he got on the plane trip down years before. The sun was low in the sky, giving the room a luminescent glow. I needed to talk to him about any plans he and my mother had made – I struggled to find the right way to say – for their final arrangements. I wanted to be sure I knew what he wanted when the time came. I fumbled around with the words until the quizzical look on his face relaxed and he seemed to understand what I was getting at. He stared down at his cards spread out on the table, a losing hand.

"I want to be cremated," he told me. "I want to burn like Donna had to burn. My poor girl–she must have suffered so much in the last moments, knowing she was burning to death and no one was coming for her. I often think of her dying from the outside in – slowly losing consciousness."

It was the only time I ever saw my father cry.

Chapter Thirteen **1957**

After the settlement with the airline, my mother saw a chance to get us out of urban apartment living and insisted on building our house with some of the proceeds. I was three when we moved to the blue house with white shutters and two-car garage.

"It's a lot of money just for a place to live," my father said.

"This is not just a place to live, it's a place to raise our girls in a better environment–out of the city."

My mother talked about the prospects of a house a little every day, until one day she suggested they take a drive. By this time, my father was getting used to the idea.

Rutgers Road was under development, with a few houses built, and several under construction. The developer met them at the end of the street. He was a fire hydrant of a man, his belly dipping slightly over the belt of his worn jeans.

"We've got one we just poured the foundation for," he told them. "You can pick all the appliances and finishing for this one yourself. A real custom job. Nice, solid construction on these houses here."

Every Sunday we went as a family to see the progress on our house. We watched it grow from a square hole in the ground, to the wood framing and finally, the paved driveway. My father took pictures with his box camera hanging from his neck in the brown leather case. He inspected every corner of the building and seemed satisfied each time that he "approved" the next phase. Hands in his pockets, he looked up toward the top of the framed roof and nodded his "ok."

My mother picked out all the gold appliances, the yellow vinyl flooring for the kitchen and the pink tile in the bathroom. The Formica counter tops only came in gray.

The house was on a quiet street that looped around to form a horseshoe. It didn't connect to any other street in the small suburban town: anyone driving into our street either lived there or was visiting someone. The neighborhood was spacious and open, with a half acre for each of the single-family homes. It was a far cry from our apartment in Elizabeth. My mother said she liked it because it was safe.

"There's no traffic at all," she told my Aunt Maxine on the phone when she described the house. "And the kids can play in the street here. Best of all, we're 25 miles from the nearest airport."

I had my own room, but I wanted to share the big room with Linda, so they put two twin beds in there for us. One of our windows looked out on the street, the other on a smaller roof overhanging the garage.

My earliest memory there has to do with a makeshift tent made from a blue tarp that my father used to collect the fall leaves. He would drag them to the edge of our backyard and burn them in a metal trashcan.

I was no more than four. Bruce and Robby, a couple of kids from the neighborhood, were visiting us with their parents. Bruce was just my age, very small and skinny. Robby was a few years older, so we did whatever he said.

We were outside behind the garage in the back of the house, far from the adults who were gathered inside in the living room. The tarp lay discarded on the ground near us. Robby was just beginning to be curious about the differences between boys and girls and cajoled me into pulling down my pants to show him. Everyone was always telling me to do that at that stage of my life, since potty training was not far behind me, so I saw no problem with it. That's when the spark of his enterprising scheme hit him, and Robby figured that the kids in the neighborhood would pay a nickel–maybe even a dime – to see me do that too. He supposed some of them would pay to have Bruce do the same thing. He said he would share his bounty with Bruce and I if we would go along. Robby hooked up the corners of the tarp from one edge of the garage roof over to the top of the rain gutter on the nearest corner of the house. He positioned Bruce and I inside and went out to hawk the show to the neighborhood.

There was a line of kids extending from our backyard to the street, and the show had only just begun when I heard my father's booming voice. He ripped open the tent door to find me standing nonchalantly with my pants around my ankles. The look in his eyes was one of disgust and seared through me, defining a shame that I did not know existed until that moment. He grabbed me under his arm like a football, carrying me out and screaming at the kids to "get the hell out of here, go the hell home NOW! Not you, Robby, I want to talk to YOU!"

Everyone scattered quickly. Bruce just picked up his pants and walked home with the rest of the crowd. I don't know if his parents ever knew what had happened that afternoon. What I remember most is that this incident was the beginning of my unsavory reputation with my father. Although he outwardly blamed the older boy, I felt his disapproval and that he deemed it somewhat my fault. I was some kind of a bad seed. My mother was the one who had the talk with me. She was very calm and assumed I was an innocent victim. She made it clear what I should and should not share with the public, and boys in particular. None of us ever spoke of it ever again.

I started flying when I was four. Giving in to a force I felt pulling at me to lift myself out of the here and now, above it all.

At the time, I wasn't aware that I could *not* fly. My confidence in my ability to leave the earth was absolute. If only I could find the right material. The right colors to lift me away into flight. From what? A whisper of dread? A hum of responsibility in my ear?

My mother's scarves were easy to find in the top drawer of her dresser. I'd watched her wrap them in fashionable knots to dress up a plain knit dress or cotton blouse. She used the accessories to seemingly expand her wardrobe beyond her modest budget. They buoyed her, and I thought they could do the same for me.

I tied four of the most luxurious, rainbow colored silks together, pulled the corners tight around my neck and jumped off the back porch. The eight concrete steps felt like an eight story building.

The wind suspended me. I held my breath. My heart pounded in my chest and I defeated gravity for a moment – before it claimed me.

The ground slapped my body flat. Blue, green, red, silk splattered over me. But, I had glimpsed freedom.

Chapter Fourteen **2005**

Down in my basement, going through the suitcase full of memorabilia, I keep thinking the next photo I turn up will be one of them at 5, or 7, or 10 years old. But, none ever materializes.

There are precious few of them as a couple before the accident. I love to look at their faces in those few photos of them – before. Before they were grabbed by tragedy. Before the unimaginable happened.

In one photo, my parents sit casually on a blanket in a park. Most likely, it's Warnanco Park in Elizabeth. My mother sits in front of him, her hand behind her to hold his. They look like someone had just surprised them with the camera. Maybe they were kissing and the photographer thought to embarrass them. They look so playful. The affection between them in the picture surprises me.

The only remnant of her unmarried life that I find in my mother's belongings is her high school autograph book. The blistered, brown charred book holds evidence of my father's romantic side. In 1934, he wrote in it:

To Flurry;
There's a word in every language
To everyone is dear;
In English 'tis forget-me-not
In French – la souvenir.
Al

That must have been just after they met, and he was on his best behavior with her. On the opposite page of the book, he later wrote another note:

To Flurry (my Wife)
May the rest of your days be happy ones – with me!
Your lover, Al

My father wrote poems to my mother for almost every occasion, and she kept most of them. They must have reminded her of the boy she fell in love with, even when she may have lost her faith in that love. His writing was his most intimate expression of the affection that he must have felt but had limited capacity to show. After the accident, just before I was born, he wrote:

Darling,
It's been so very, very difficult
To speak my every thought;
To speak of all the heartache
That fate to us has wrought.

To lose so much and yet retain
Your love, so dear and true;
Has held my faith together –
Has helped to see me through.

You're the essence of my being,
My moon and star and sun;
Please remember sweetheart
We're not finished –just begun!

I love you, Al

There is so little physical evidence of their early days together that I have to rely on the stories I was told.

When they were first married, my father had his milk delivery route in the morning, the pharmacy job in the afternoons. He would leave the house at 4 am every day, whistling as always. He'd hop in the small white dairy truck to make the rounds with fresh milk and cream on cold winter mornings and sultry summer dawns, remembering the special orders and the ones that needed to pay up.

My father's pharmacy job is legend. Firstly, there was the story of him running bootleg whiskey all over town. Then, later, he helped the owner discover that an employee was stealing from him by collecting on credit from customers and not turning in the money. He came home every night with stories of the people on his route and his encounters in the drug store.

My mother was the hands-on caregiver for her mother, who, during the early days of their marriage, lived with them in their small apartment. Her care was difficult because of diabetes, and later a colostomy. There were daily insulin injections, and tending to the colostomy for years, not to mention keeping a kosher home for her strictly orthodox mother. When Grandma Schlesinger died, "after hanging in just long enough to hold you in her arms," my mother swore she would never keep kosher again. "Too many dishes, too damn much trouble!"

Later, when my mother developed diabetes in her sixties, the memory of caring for her mother was what fed her fears. Her mother wound up with her legs amputated, and my mother vowed she would "go out of this world with all the parts God gave me."

A photo I come across in the pile is of my father strolling down a New York City street with his sister Bess. It shows the happy-go-lucky version – a man I wish I had known. Dressed to the nines in a dapper pin-stripe suit, he would be bouncing each step on the balls of his feet, barely touching the ground. Looking at his carefree younger self, I'm glad my father had no premonition of what was to come.

All I know about their past is from stories sprinkled out over the years like so many breadcrumbs. My father's stories about his childhood had either a punch line or a warning.

A story my father liked to tell was about when he and his brother Heimi were riding in a carriage and a couple of boys called after them "kikes, get out of here." Heimi, a usually calm boy, jumped from the carriage and "beat the crap out of those boys! We never had any trouble from them again." This story made me scared of being Jewish, or at least of telling people that I was.

Heimi had a hole in his heart. When he was a teenager, the family heard that the air in Ohio would be better for him, so they packed up and moved to Akron. The air didn't prove to be any better there than in New Jersey and Heimi died anyway. He's buried "somewhere near Akron."

Life is short was the lesson from this story. We have no control.

In my favorite photo of my mother, she is wearing her white, wide brimmed picture book hat that I coveted. She is glancing back distractedly over her shoulder in what I think of as her starlet pose.

My parents had eight years alone as a married couple before having a child. It was difficult for my mother to conceive, she told me when I was trying to have my own baby. I also wondered if my father's tendency to be physically distant and unaffectionate had something to do with it. It shouldn't have surprised me then when I later learned that my father's parents barely spoke when he was growing up.

There are a few photos of them when they were a young family of three, with baby Donna. One has my mother, my father and Donna dressed in their winter coats standing primly in front of their apartment building. The frozen moment of completeness seems as permanent as the building's brick facade.

Next to this picture is one of the four of us – Mom, Dad, Linda and me – without Donna. To me, this is our family, but I wonder what my parents saw when they looked at this photo.

Photos of my father holding Donna and one of him holding me at the same age show a different kind of father in each. Holding Donna, he has a youthful expression of "look at my baby–she's mine" and holds her away from him. He's young and trim with his full head of black hair. Holding me, he keeps me close to his cheek with his arm pulling me next to him, a serious expression on his more mature face. His lowered, scrunched eyebrows are what I remember most.

Donna and Linda

Linda and me

Two other pictures mirror each other, as if the second photo was staged to be an exact replica of the first, creating a photographic continuity of the family. The first is of Donna holding Linda as a newborn on her lap in front of her, arms protectively clasped around the baby. The second is of Linda holding me in the same pose, her pinched scarred arms tightly around me. Her badly burned left leg sticks out of her skirt in front of her. The love in their eyes is the same.

It's a strange comfort to see the two pictures together. One of the only connections I have between all of us sisters.

Chapter Fifteen
JANUARY 22, 1952
DAY OF THE CRASH
7:45 AM

My father parked his car behind Goerke's department store, waved to the attendant and walked toward Broad Street. Goerke's and Levy Bros. department stores were the signature stores of downtown Elizabeth. His older sister, Ada worked at Levy Bros. and he stopped in to see her now and then. Down the street was Woolworth's 5 & 10.

The Rite Aid pharmacy blinked its neon sign across the street. The Con Edison showroom was full of "modern" gleaming white stoves and refrigerators. Around the corner, you could listen to 45's in a special booth in the record store before you chose one.

At the glass door of Goldblatt Jewelers, he stopped to choose the right key from the large set jingling in his pocket, turned the key in the lock and heard the satisfying click. Standing in the doorway for a moment, my father surveyed the quiet store in the subdued morning sunlight coming in through the front windows. A spotlight on his day. Dust particles did pirouettes in the refracted light over the long showcases.

Locking the door behind him, my father set into his usual routine. He uncovered the showcases, placed jewelry artistically in the outside windows and checked the cash register, whistling as he went through his checklist.

After the store was ready for the day, my father opened and relocked the door, then went next door to Pamel's Luncheonette for coffee and a pack of Pall Mall cigarettes. Pamel's had a row of red plastic upholstered booths and a lunch counter with a real soda jerk that made sodas to order.

This day, Rita, the waitress he knew for years, smiled and sat down with him to kibitz for a few minutes while he drank his coffee and had another cigarette before opening the store.

Chapter Sixteen
1959

At around age 5, I dressed like a cowboy and climbed trees. My father began to call me "my son Judy." Linda was more interested in having a girlfriend over to sit in her room and listen to 45's on her portable record player.

My father and I played baseball in the backyard until one fateful day when he hit me square in the nose while he was showing me how to catch a fastball. At first, he started yelling at me that I didn't keep my eye on the ball and my glove in front of my face like he taught me. But when he saw that I was bleeding he came running over. My nose was spurting blood so hard we couldn't make it stop. My mother heard the commotion and ran out from the kitchen with a towel for my nose and ushered me inside with a stern look at my father. That was the end of our playing baseball, and the start of my father treating me differently. Maybe he saw me as suddenly fragile, brought to the reality of my female status so abruptly, and was afraid to hurt me with rough 'boy' type play – afraid to have another child of his hurt in any way. I only knew that we stopped being pals.

After that, I must have been 9 or 10, I was drawn to the boys in my neighborhood. Playing with boys was much more interesting than what the girls always wanted to do. Tea parties and dressing up Barbie was not my idea of a good time. Two brothers, Richy and Tommy, who lived across the street would let me come over to play army, football, or baseball with them. They treated me like one of the guys. I liked that they didn't give me extra points in kickball, or throw a ball softer to me. But, they were pretty tough guys, and it turned out I was not. One day when I came home bruised from playing a game of tackle football with them, my mother forbade me to play with them anymore. She tried to foster some relationships with the girls in my neighborhood, which didn't work out very well.

At gatherings at our house, the men usually wound up in the living room and the women in the kitchen. Kitchen duty was just an excuse for the women to get away to talk among themselves, about children, cooking and clothes. I would gravitate to where the men were gathered, trying to infiltrate their male world. I'd hang back in the corner of the room, nursing a piece of cake one crumb at a time. I wanted to listen to him talk about his business, politics and what he thought about world events, the way I never heard him talk to my mother and us. The men talked differently than the women and were not afraid to argue or disagree. I liked their frank talk better than the women's, who avoided the sensitive topics they had between them. The men's discussions held clues about the larger world – and my father.

Chapter Seventeen
1960

It seemed that my parents had always been prepared for some kind of disaster. Canned goods lined my mother's pantry in case of blizzards, or worse – war. We didn't have a bomb shelter, but we knew neighbors that did. When my father held my hand crossing the street he let me know that even if a car waves me on, I shouldn't trust them, I should let them go first. My mother would check each restaurant and shop we went to for the emergency back entrance.

When I was six I witnessed my first real emergency situation when Hurricane Donna hit us. It felt like the roof was blowing off the house.

My mother warned me to stay away from the window where I stood watching our street fill with fallen trees, a window awning – even some patio chairs and tables. My father took us down the cellar when the storm got bad "just to be safe."

My mother made hot chocolate with little marshmallows. My father got candles and a flashlight so that we could play cards.

Later, when the storm had truly been spent, my father went outside in the backyard to check on the damage while Linda and I watched out the kitchen window. It was a real mess. Branches and leaves were all over the place. Our clothesline was lying clear across the yard, its metal arms at its side and lines tangled like long fingers.

Then he saw a branch a little bigger than the others, with the roots still attached. He stopped to examine it closely, shook his head and carried it into the garage.

With the sun back out the next day, I followed my father outside to clean things up. He stood the clothesline back up and secured it into the ground. Then he brought that little branch out from the garage and studied it for a moment. He looked up at me like he had a great idea.

"Let's plant it," he said. "It will be our Donna tree–from Hurricane Donna. We'll always remember, right, Juicy?"

We walked the yard to pick just the right spot for the new tree.

"We need to give it plenty of room," he told me. "This is going to be the biggest tree in the yard someday. You'll help me nurse it back to health."

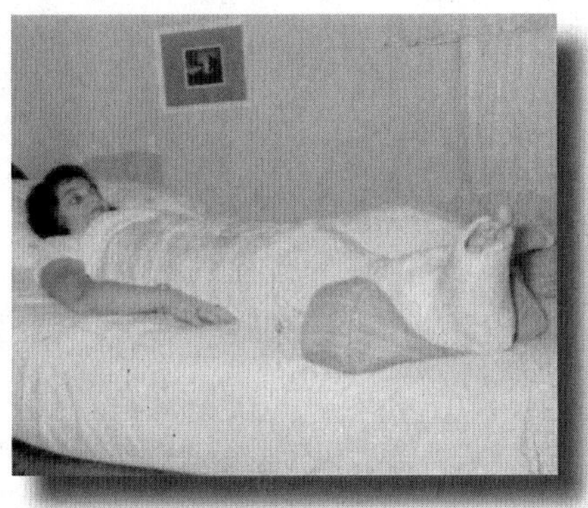

I was also six when Linda had the surgery where they broke both of her legs to set them right again. I remember hoping that afterward she'd be able to ride her bike with me, or go for a walk on the beach in the summer.

Linda's roommate in the hospital, Chi Chi, was from Brazil. Her leg was mangled in a motorcycle accident, and her mother brought her to New York in an attempt to save the leg. Chi Chi's leg, however, was ultimately amputated.

The mothers of the girls got them each a Spanish-English/English-Spanish dictionary. The first word they looked up was pain, *dolor.*

They made up their own sign language for important things–like "change the TV channel," "I'm hungry," "It hurts," and "When do we get out of this dump?"

Between them, they had one good leg, Linda said. But they both used it. When Linda needed a bedpan quick, Chi Chi would hop over to get it for her.

As the two mothers got to know each other, my mother learned that the trip from South America and the extended stay in the U.S. was a considerable hardship on her new friend. She was running out of funds and had nowhere to stay, so my mother brought her home for the remainder of Chi Chi's hospitalization.

"Another stray," my father muttered when she broke the news. The time before it was their housekeeper who ran into hard times.

Linda told me that no one had prepared her for the pain she had after this surgery – it was the worst she had ever had. She concocted her own method for dealing with it. With absolute quiet, she could increase her tolerance by closing her eyes and analyzing what she was feeling–exactly where the sharpest point was, how it intensified, and why it was happening. Was it less than yesterday? If it was, that meant it would be less tomorrow. Somehow, telling herself she could stand it, helped more than trying to kid herself into believing it didn't hurt. My mother used to try to distract her from the pain, but eventually she understood, and gave her the quiet she needed to concentrate.

I knew my eye surgery didn't compare with anything Linda had been through. She was a scrappy foot soldier, and I was a turncoat running for cover from any hint of discomfort. She was valiant, I was a whiner.

When they brought her home, the ambulance pulled up with its red lights on and I ran to stand at the top of the stairs. I had on the nurse uniform that my mother got me especially to greet Linda. I loved the little white hat and the white dress with big pockets. I imagined waiting on Linda, carrying cookies for her in those pockets. A blue cape finished off the outfit, making me feel like I could fly around the house to bring Linda anything she needed. I felt powerful in that costume, like I could heal my sister with just the right smile.

When they started to unload her from the back of the ambulance, I saw the wide white cast from her waist to her toes, with a bar between her legs. It took three men to carry her, but when they got to the front door they stopped. My mother looked over at my father, who had that worry crease in his forehead, and they both ran down the stairs. Linda, in her cast, couldn't fit through.

"I can take the door off the hinges," my father told the men.

"She may not fit even then. We may have to turn her on her side."

My mother took a deep breath. From what I could see, Linda looked pretty worried and scared, so I gave her one of my healing smiles. She smiled back.

My father got his tools, unscrewed something and lifted the door off its hinges. They finally turned her sideways, with one leg up, one down to fit through the opening. Her feet came in first and I watched to see her head come in. When they turned her right-side up, her cheeks were wet.

Since my mother needed to sleep in the extra bed in Linda's room, I had to move to my own room for a while. This was a grave disappointment to me. Having missed my sister for a month already, I now had to give up sharing the room with her too. We wouldn't get to talk at night and try to listen to my parents talking in their room next door.

It was winter, and in the next few days we saw our first real snowfall. Linda could see the top of the lower roof, over the garage, from her bed and I caught her staring out at the snow-covered surface.

"I would really like to *feel* that snow," she said.

I went to the kitchen and got one of my mother's metal mixing bowls. Then I got my jacket and mittens and went back to Linda's room.

"What are you doing?"

"You'll see."

I opened up the window and the screen underneath, crawled out on the roof and scooped some snow into the bowl. When I started back in, I saw my mother coming through the door.

She didn't yell like I was afraid she would. She just took the bowl from my hands as I climbed back in and put it on top of Linda's cast on her tummy.

My mother pulled up a chair next to the bed and I sat on the legs of the cast. The three of us each grabbed a handful of the cold icy stuff, rolled it into a ball and stuck them all together in the bowl. It ended up a perfect miniature of the snowman we always built on the front lawn with raisins for eyes, a small piece of carrot for the nose and a funny hat my mother made out of an old red sock. I crawled back on the roof to put our snowman where Linda could see it from her bed.

Chapter Eighteen **2005**

I'm getting more disciplined now with this 'project' as I have started to call it. Mornings I will find one pile of notes or news clips and re-read them until they jar a memory from my past. Then, I'll write a page or two from that memory. Afternoons, I'll review and re-write the piece. The next day, I either add it to my growing file called "The Book" on my computer–or trash it if it's awful. Either way, I usually wind up with a revelation I didn't expect.

My office is getting crowded with notes hung on my bulletin board, or scotch taped to the edges of my windowsill. Photos of my parents, my sisters and myself are tacked up where I see them each time I look up from my computer. I took pictures of the rebuilt neighborhood when I went to visit the crash site, and those are hanging next to a photo of the burned out building from 1952, and one of the split-level house I grew up in.

Today, I'm starting with more notes from my mother. They are spread out randomly on my kitchen table. It takes me a while to decipher each piece, with her notoriously bad handwriting. Her writing was so bad that she had printed most of her notes in block letters. The more I read, the more I see that she had a burning desire to tell the story, and I'm hoping I can do it justice for her. Although

I know that some of the story will be information she never told me – and might not have wanted me to tell.

I've skimmed over these notes before, but never really gave them attention. Now, they look different to me as possible puzzle pieces. In my mother's stark accounts of that awful afternoon, she remembered her horror over and over again:

I can still hear my little girl's scream – a cry I shall never ever forget and the only cry in her short life I was unable to answer.

The devastation of the loss of our beautiful seven-year-old daughter, coupled with the heart breaking condition of Linda was more than any human being could bear all at once. But two people as close as my husband and I could cry to each other and lend one another support. When we met Donna's friends who were growing up and getting on with their lives, we felt Donna was cheated, and Linda was cheated of a normal life. And so were we.

I'm surprised to read about my parents' closeness in my mother's notes and wonder if it was more of a wish than a fact. It's one of many ill-shaped fragments of the story that I begin to realize won't fit into my version of their puzzle, or my own.

My mother and father surely must have had fortitude to make it through such an ordeal together, but I remember their fighting most vividly. Much of the time it was about money. Always trying to make ends meet, and the undercurrent resentment of not getting an adequate settlement from the airline for Linda's ongoing care. My father was always the affable joke teller when we had guests, but his jokes were often aimed at my mother. And, I never saw my father put an arm around his wife, reach out to hold her hand or steal a kiss at the kitchen sink.

Thinking of my parents' complicated relationship, I wonder whether my father's inattention was an impetus for my mother looking elsewhere for validation as a woman, and I am starting to recognize a similar pattern in my own life. There was a persistent rumor about an affair with our 'Uncle Jack.' He was Sheila, Donna's best friend's father, who had been visiting on the day of the crash and who had also been terribly burned in the accident. Jack was a balding, soft-spoken, gentle man with heavy black-rimmed glasses. He was taller and broader than my father. Uncle Jack would stoop over slightly whenever he talked to me when I was a child, to get down to my size. Along with Sheila, he had an older son, Michael. Jack owned a successful sporting goods store.

When we moved from our apartment to our new house, Jack bought a house on the next street over. He was a member of the swim club we joined to get Linda the swimming exercise she needed for her legs. We went there every day in the summers for quite a few years, and Jack was ever-present. For a while, I remember he and his wife (also named Florence) would come over often for coffee in the evenings. Then we only saw Jack by himself, usually when he brought Linda and I presents. My father would nearly growl when Jack showed up at our house. I also remember occasionally stopping by his store.

Stuck in a yellowed envelope between the pages of one of my parents' old photo albums, I find three wrinkled tickets to Radio City Music Hall. When I was eight, my mother packed our pj's, underwear and extra clothes and called a taxi that drove us to the bus stop – without my father. The bus ride to New York City was only about a half hour.

I asked Linda why my father wasn't coming with us.

"I think Mommy's mad at him."

"We'll go the Empire State Building today, and I got us tickets for Radio City tomorrow," my mother told us while we unpacked our suitcases at the hotel.

Later, we went to lunch at the Horn n' Hardart Automat. I loved that you could see all the different food behind the little glass doors and pick whatever you wanted, then put the right number of nickels in the slot and slide open the little door. Everything was wrapped in wax paper. As soon as one thing came out, another went in. I saw people working behind the glass when I took my peanut butter and jelly sandwich.

My Tiny Tears doll with the wooden head came along with me. She was a great comfort. Just the week before I had cracked her head open on the basement steps. My father brought her to his doll 'operating room' and fixed her. He painted her head to have brown hair just like mine. Thinking of that made me want him with us even more.

Over the next two days, my mother was on the phone a lot talking to my father. I tried to hear, but she pulled the phone into the bathroom.

After Radio City, I asked when we were going home.

"Soon," she said, which told me nothing. "Soon" could literally mean hours, days or weeks.

In a couple of days we did go home. My father was waiting at the bus stop, smoking a cigarette with his lips all squeezed together. When he saw us, he threw down the butt like a dart and stamped it under his foot. He ran over to us and hugged my mother for a long time.

My father's writings are in a different folder. There are fewer pages, the sparse information is written in his neat, almost calligraphic pen. His notes to me focus on getting the facts straight … *that may be pertinent to whatever story you might write.*

He wrote about the other two crashes that occurred within the four-month period surrounding ours: one in December of 1951, and one in March of 1952.

When a plane hit in March of '52, he and my mother were still homeless from the accident–staying in a hotel.

We were preparing for bed when we heard on the radio that another plane crash had just taken place not far from the hotel. We dressed and went to the hospital to relieve Linda's nurses in case they would be needed.

My father's notes to me are filled with contradictions, a veritable fugue of internal conflict. In one version, he muses about the miracles of that day: my mother wearing a flammable apron that never caught fire and Linda's survival against the odds. Other times he rants on the injustice of a God that would let this happen to his family.

He was clearly touched, though, by the outpouring of the community:

We were completely wiped out except for the clothing on my back, but the response from the public and generosity of relatives was, for me, overwhelming. Calls came in from people in all walks of life, offering donations of blood, skin for grafts, and clothing. One Elizabeth policeman and another good friend took up a collection to help us in the immediate emergency and we were able to buy clothing we needed just then.

My sister's notes tell the story of her many surgeries, of friends that saw her through, of how she struggled to fit in as she got older.

Then, there were the thinly disguised love notes to me from all three:

Our youngest was our joy.

You gave me a reason to escape the pressures of the outside world.

The most precious gift I ever received, my baby sister.

One of God's special children.

Chapter Nineteen
JANUARY 22, 1952
Day of the Crash
9:00 AM

Dr. Cohen lifted Linda's tiny chin upward to see her face in the light, turning her cheek from side to side to examine her. It tickled and she giggled at his touch.

"It's a very minor procedure to remove a birthmark like this. It's only a discoloration, no raised skin or deformation. I can do it on an outpatient basis. Very quick, very routine," he told my mother of the strawberry mark on Linda's right cheek. She said she would discuss it with her husband and get back to the doctor soon.

Linda was so pretty, my mother thought, it would be a shame for the birthmark to mar her face. Appearances mattered. It could affect her whole life, even who she married or what kind of job she got.

After the doctor appointment, my mother and Linda walked to Broad Street to look in the shops and get a bite to eat. Even on this dreary day, my mother was in no hurry to go back to the small apartment. She planned to stop in and see my father on the way. He never went out for lunch, so she would pick up a sandwich for him.

Halfway to Broad Street Linda was tired, so my mother hoisted her up and balanced her on her hip for the few blocks to Woolworth's. At the double glass doors, Linda jumped down and pulled my mother by the hand to the pet department to watch the goldfish and the parakeets. Then they went to look at the rolls of cloth for material for a new housedress my mother planned to sew for herself.

Crossing the street, they looked through the window of Goldblatt's and saw my father in conversation with a customer. Knowing better than to interrupt him, my mother headed straight to Pamel's. She and Linda took a booth in the middle of the shop and ordered a grilled cheese sandwich with fries, coffee and a glass of milk.

"She's getting so big, and so adorable," Rita said as she delivered their meal.

"I know, they grow up so fast. I really love this age. We're having that birthmark removed from her cheek. We just went to the doctor."

"Oh, I didn't even notice it."

My mother ordered a corned beef on rye to go for my father, and told Rita to put it all on his bill.

"No problem, Flurry. So nice to see you and the little one. You'll have to bring Donna around. I haven't seen her in so long."

"You won't recognize her, Rita. She's gotten so grown up. Seven going on seventeen! Here's the latest photo of her," my mother took out a photo from her wallet.

"Beautiful–a really beautiful girl," Rita smiled.

Chapter Twenty 1961 - 1963

My mother kept all her hats, which were just going out of style at that time, in their original cardboard hatboxes on the top shelf of her walk-in closet. I knew the white one that I loved was in the tan box with the brown trim and red ribbon keeping it closed.

When she dressed up and wore it to go out with my father, I thought she looked like a movie star – only prettier. It was those times I remembered him looking at her differently, and maybe even putting his arm around her when they went out to the car.

I was seven when I got into her closet and found the step stool tucked in the corner and used it to reach the hat. Gingerly, I untied the worn, wrinkled ribbon and popped open the box. Now, I knew I was in deep. The hatboxes were strictly off limits to little hands. Between glances over my shoulder to be sure I wasn't found out, I dug my hand into the deep layers of yellowed tissue paper that cushioned the precious headpiece. It let out a loud crackle that sounded to me like a siren calling attention to my crime.

All the adults were downstairs in the living room with some friends. Linda was playing the organ and my father was singing. I was jealous of their musical duo. It was like they had a secret language. I didn't play an instrument yet, and I didn't know the tunes to the songs they sang together. My father never asked me to sing with them, or teach me the songs, and didn't notice that I felt left out.

The hat looked great on me when I modeled it in my mother's full-length mirror, but I needed a whole outfit if I was going to steal the scene downstairs and grab away my father's attention. I spotted my mother's blue and white polka dot dress and I pulled it down from the hanger and stepped into it. I didn't need to bother with the back zipper to get it up over my head and shoulders. I was practicing my dance and strut, when I heard my mother coming up the stairs.

At first I thought she was mad. She looked like she was going to yell at me, but she changed her mind and she came over and hugged me. My mother was the queen of hugs. Warm and tight and smelling like flowers, she always held on for an extra minute that made you know she meant it.

"What's my pretty girl gotten into now?" she asked.

I didn't answer because I didn't think there was anything I could say that would help. Usually, it just made things worse when I was in trouble, so I just smiled and twirled the big skirt around to show her how I looked.

"Beautiful honey! But you need some jewelry with that dress."

She took out a giant string of pearls from her jewelry box and put them around my neck. They hung down almost to my knees, but I was pleased when I looked over at the mirror. She left me there gazing at myself and went back to her company.

I thought I needed one more thing, so I went back into the closet and got her shiny black high heels. They were hard to walk in, but I could do it if I walked on my ankles. Lipstick was the last thing I put on, bright red, from my mother's makeup table in the corner.

Walking down the stairs I was a little wobbly, but I got into the middle of the living room without falling. My aim was to show my father how beautiful I was, that I was the daughter he should pay attention to now. I pranced in and started to sashay to the music.

But when I turned around, he wasn't smiling. He had been leaning on top of the organ, but stood up straight after my dance and held his hand across his forehead like it was falling apart. His lips squeezed tight, and his eyebrows creased. He glanced over at Linda and then me, but spoke first to my mother.

"Flurry, what is she in to now? She's got hold of all your stuff," he said like he thought I couldn't hear him. "Can't you control her? She's too young to be dressing up like that. Geez! Go take Mommy's dress off young lady, and wash your face!"

I have to believe my father had no idea of the devastating effect of his words. It was later that I understood to praise me as pretty in front of my scarred sister was something he had decided early on never to do. I ripped off the dress and ran up the stairs.

The first time I ran away from home I was eight. I packed up a bologna sandwich on white, a couple of Twinkies and a carton of chocolate milk in a sheet and threw it over my shoulder like I'd seen in the movies. My mother let me go, probably thinking I wouldn't get far with only a bologna sandwich for sustenance. When I got to the center of town, I sat on a bench to eat my lunch, then went back home again. I remember her waiting at the door.

Nobody used to notice when I went to the garage, got on my bike and disappeared for hours at a time. I knew every street, all the short cuts and back roads in town. The dirt path through the woods had a quiet place to stop to sit on a tree stump and eat an apple. Or, I might go to town to the Corner Sweet Shop for a coke. But more often, I'd just ride by myself to feel free on my own – every turn down every street my own choice.

At the time, Linda was 13 or 14 and didn't want me around much. She locked the door to her room when her friends were over. I could pick the lock, which I sometimes did, but that didn't really endear her to me. She would just kick me out and yell for my mother. Sometimes we were friends like we used to be, but other times I truly thought she hated me. She would kid around, but the jokes would sometimes have a bite to them. She'd say things like, "You even got the good hair in the family." There was nothing I could say to her joking accusations, and nothing I could ever do to even the score.

Meanwhile, my parents were constantly planning our lives around Linda's hospital visits. They'd be planning the next surgery for June when it was only September. I didn't allow myself to feel resentful.

When I was 11, I wrote to Barnum & Bailey's Circus about joining up. I wanted to go to clown school – right away. I wanted to

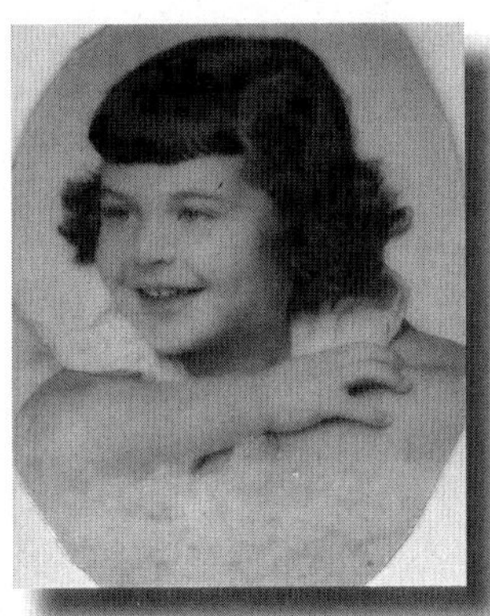

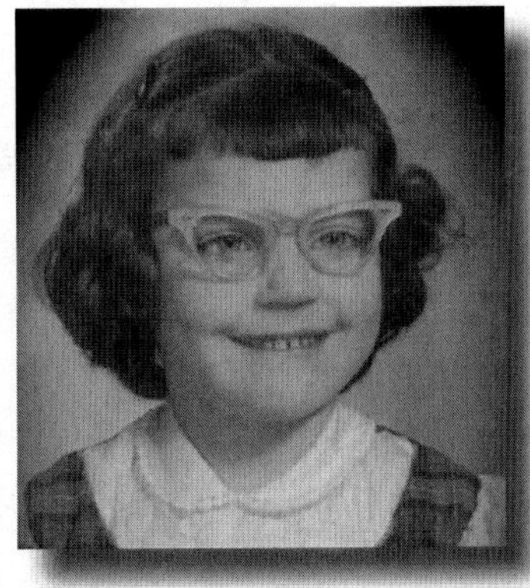

learn to make people laugh like my father always did. I saw that it made people love him, and I thought my clowning might make him love me. I waited for a long time for a reply, and then forgot about it. My mistake, I found out later, was asking my mother to mail the letter. She never did.

I looked like her. Or she looked like me, but nobody ever mentioned it.

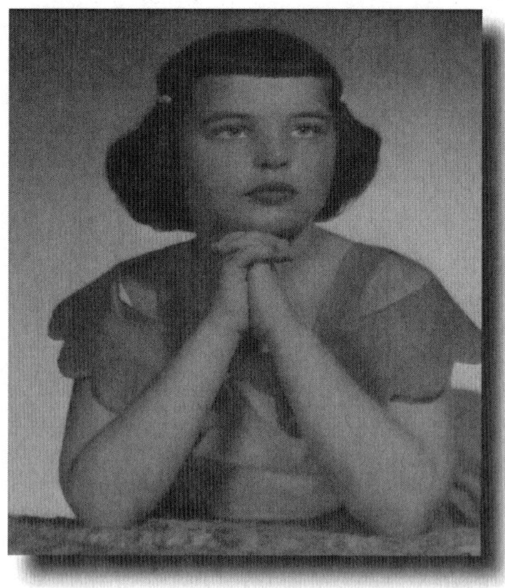

I was nine and looking for my father to come help me with a picture I was painting. My mother said he was in their bedroom reading, but he wasn't here. I went over to his side of their big bed, which was really two beds pushed together. His nightstand was crowded with two books, his clock radio that he listened to at night and his black rimmed reading glasses. I sat down on the bed and looked up at the wall full of photos that I had never taken notice of before.

For a minute, I thought they were pictures of me, but they were all her.

In the center was the formal 11 x 14 portrait taken just before she died. She was seven in the photo, although she looked at least thirteen. Her apricot silk sundress had off-the-shoulder scalloped sleeves. Her chestnut hair was curled in a pageboy, the sides held in place with white barrettes, bangs cut straight and high on her forehead. Just like mine. She leaned lightly on her elbows with her hands clasped in front of her. If you looked hard enough, at her thoughtful expression, you could see the woman she might have become.

My mother walked in as I was scrutinizing each picture and she sat down on the bed next to me. She put her arm around me and we didn't say anything for a while. Then she started to tell me about the photos.

She pointed to the picture of Donna at six months old with her chubby cheeks filling the frame.

"Her legs were too fat for her to walk," my mother explained, admitting that she doted on Donna, maybe even overfeeding her first child so much that it delayed walking.

"She really didn't need to get up for anything," she chuckled.

She told me that she had just turned three when the photo was taken of her with short, curly hair, sitting primly. My mother stopped when she got to the one that looked most like me, of Donna in a casual pose, leaning both arms on a blanket in front of her. She gave me a squeeze.

All the faces of my sister. The daughter lost to them. But she was there every morning when they first put their feet on the ground and every night when they closed their eyes. Not forgotten, never really gone.

After the crash, my father told me he was determined to recover some of the old photos that were lost in the fire. When he called the photographer to get a replacement photo of the last picture taken of Donna, my mother fought with him.

"It will just remind us more. Every single day," she said.

"I want it! It was a beautiful picture of her!"

My father went to the rest of the family to collect photos they had kept of Donna, to add to his memorial wall.

My Uncle Art and Aunt Ruth both sent a few small photos of Donna along with some of my mother and father with her, and of Linda before the accident.

My father spread them out on the kitchen table with some frames, scissors and tape. When my mother walked in, she accused him, "What are you doing? I hope you aren't planning to hang those."

At this, my father raised his voice.

"Isn't it enough that she's gone? That all traces of her have been erased from our lives? We don't have a doll she played with, or a sweater she wore, or even a crayon picture she made in school! Can't we at least have something of her in our house?"

My father continued matching each picture to the perfect round gilded frame, or square black one with his artistic eye. He held each photo for a moment, staring at his girl, before deciding how to shape and fit her into place, taping each image squarely onto a photo mat before securing it behind glass. When he was done with the framing, he knew better than to hang them in the living room.

That's how he chose the spot in their bedroom, on his side of the bed, where my mother could avert her eyes if she wanted to. He centered the large portrait and was positioning the picture hooks for the others when my mother walked in on him. He stopped the hammer in mid-air to turn to her, his eyes pleading for this one concession. She nodded to him slightly, turned and walked away.

After my mother's explanation of the photos, my father joined us on the bed, sitting on the other side of me. He glanced up at Donna on the wall over us and leaned over to pick up the one photo of me on his nightstand – a 2" x 3" snapshot in a white metal frame. In the photo I was sporting Donna's same pageboy hairstyle. Only my blue-rimmed glasses, and my lazy left eye, made it me.

"My favorite of you," he said.

Chapter Twenty-One
JANUARY 22 1952
Day of the Crash
12:00 PM

My father was showing a Bulova watch to a man in a black overcoat, but he was thinking about the corned beef on rye that my mother had brought him, and that waited for him in the back room.

My mother was back on the bus with Linda, headed for home. It had been a full morning already and she was looking forward to getting Linda down to take a nap. My grandmother would need her lunch, and then she could relax for a couple of hours.

Donna was having lunch in the school cafeteria at a crowded table of her friends. They were swapping apples for cookies, peanut butter sandwiches for tuna. Donna ate the cream cheese and jelly sandwich my mother had packed for her, and bought a carton of milk.

Meanwhile, Flight 6780 was about to leave Buffalo airport. There were stops scheduled in Rochester and Syracuse before its return to Newark. Because the weather was uncertain, with a cold mist forming patches of fog along the way, the pilot would have to use instruments in order to land safely. In case of a turn in the weather, or other problems he might encounter, there were alternate airports listed in Albany, New York and Connecticut. The flight lifted off at 12:14 and landed first in Rochester at 12:37. It took off again at 12:58.

Chapter Twenty-Two **2005**

I want to take a full-fledged research trip to Elizabeth and present the proposition to David and Justin to come with me. David is amenable, as he usually is, and blocks out some time from his job. David has seen how I've been changed by the death of my parents, and understands on a deep level my quest for answers through writing this story. I feel lucky to have such a partner, that cares to listen and follows up his caring words with actions. We've talked a lot lately about my writing and the conflicts I'm having with telling the story. Like how I feel a responsibility to my parents to tell the story they would have wanted, to tell my own story as I lived it and to uncover the truths that may have alluded me. It's a high wire act, and at times I am caught between their truth and my own. Do I tell about my mother's affair, for example? My sister says it's disrespectful. But it explains so much to me about my parents' relationship and the effect it had on my future choices in men. How much do I tell about my sister Linda's life without intruding on her privacy? And, how about my past husbands? Should I change their names?

David is a wonderful sounding board and helps me think through many of my issues. From the start, he's been my number one cheerleader.

When I discuss spending a day or two in New Jersey with Justin, he shrugs and packs an extra book in case he gets bored.

The Elizabeth Public Library on Broad Street is a stately old building with thick stone walls and Romanesque columns guarding the entrance.

I walk slowly up the concave marble steps, where surely Donna had walked once or twice. I wander through the children's section, wondering if she sat on these same wooden benches while my mother read to her. My phantom sister seems alive here in this place.

We are pointed to the research area of the library, up on the third floor. The librarian there takes a moment to register my request, looks over her black half-glasses and points to the 1952 archives.

There are lots of records to go through, all on old-fashioned microfiche, for *The Elizabeth Star Ledger, The Daily Journal* and *The New York Times* for the weeks following January 22, 1952. Luckily, there are three microfiche machines we can use. We each station ourselves at one and start working the knobs slowly enough to scan the articles, maneuvering dials to zoom in on tiny type and murky photos, scrounging for quarters to print out pages. When any of us finds something related to the crash, we shout out to the others – "wow", "look at this", "I can't believe this." We are getting dirty looks from the librarian, who has her index finger positioned resolutely over her pursed lips.

Justin doesn't know that much about the plane crash. I have probably sheltered him from it just the way my parents tried to shelter me. He knows his Aunt Linda is scarred, had operations in the past and some recently as a result. But he knows nothing about the effect the accident had on my life. That may be one of the reasons I'm writing the story. To give my son more a sense of who I am.

David and I have talked about how the accident may have shaped me. He knows everything about my first three marriages and why I believe they didn't work, but we haven't been able to draw a straight line from the crash to the issues I had with my previous husbands. It's another reason I think he's so supportive of me trying to write my way out of my confusion and put a name to my men troubles. Though I've done a lot of personal work to understand my relationships, we both feel knowing more about this connection to my past will help protect us from whatever has reared up in my psyche before. In his heart I think David feels I just wasn't with the right man before – and now I am.

In one newspaper story, I discover that it wasn't a fireman, as my mother said, who had held her back from the burning building. It was a man named Henry Shubecz, who had been driving on South Street, crossing Williamson, when the plane crashed in front of him. He jumped from his car to my mother's door, saw the intensity of the blaze and held her back–saving her life. For a moment, I think about this stranger who intersected with our lives at the critical juncture. Who was he? What was he doing there? Where was he going? And, did he ever know how his act had reverberated through the next generations of my family? That in saving Linda, he made the lives of her two daughters possible as well as her two grandsons. That in saving my mother, he saved me too?

Articles in *The Star Ledger* describe an uproar in the Elizabeth community – investigations of the crash, the airport and the aircraft.

A photo shows the jury from the criminal investigation scrambling through the rubble on a field trip to see the crash site, kicking through the remnants of my family home. Did they come upon Donna's doll? Linda's tinker toys? Or kick aside scraps of treasured photos that my mother tried to replace for the next 50 years?

Newark Airport was closed on February 11, 1952, but the U.S. Air force reopened it for military use after six weeks, and for commercial flights shortly thereafter.

Each new detail allows me to share in the tragedy, but I am still left with the philosophic questions:

Why this plane?

Why this house?

Why this child?

My New-Agey friends talk about learning something from each lifetime. Choosing your own circumstances for each successive life in order to learn what you need for your soul's progress.

I like this idea, but I can never swallow that Donna chose to be killed by a plane dropping from the sky when she was seven. Or that Linda chose to be scarred and in pain much of her life. Or even that I chose my role.

No, I do not believe these to be part of any master plan. We are on our own. We make decisions that determine our survival each and every day. We are at the whim of every decision made by every other human on the planet and at the mercy of forces of nature, whirling through this life without so much as a twist-tie holding us steady. The more I read of the accident, the more I am convinced:

Anything can happen.

Chapter Twenty-Three
JANUARY 22, 1952
DAY OF THE CRASH
1:00 PM

Donna was back in her 2nd grade classroom after lunch period watching a film of President Truman signing the G.I. Bill of Rights for Korean War veterans. She was thinking of the brave soldiers, and pictures she'd seen of the injured.

My father was in the back room of the store at his old oak jewelers bench that was crammed with his accounting books, adding machine and receipts. He had spread out the bag from his lunch over the top of the mess to protect the papers and opened up the butcher paper to retrieve his sandwich. He could keep an eye on the front of the store from this vantage and pop out to the counter if a customer walked in. Biting into the sandwich, he felt a surge of affection for his wife, who thought to bring him lunch.

My mother and Linda walked the two blocks from the bus stop to home. Linda was getting sleepy, and my mother let her walk the last distance to tire her out fully for her nap. They climbed the steep stairs to their second floor apartment. My mother peeled off Linda's coat and her own and hung them both in the hall closet.

Captain Reid was checking the weather at Syracuse airport. He may have been worried about the fog and cold rain, but by the time he landed in Syracuse at 1:34 pm, visibility had improved and he had no problem at all. In fact, the flight was routine to the point of boredom.

Chapter Twenty-Four
1963 - 1972

My mother had not been out of bed all day. She was still in her flowered nightgown. The room was stuffy and close. She wasn't reading a book, watching TV or even sleeping. On better days, she would be waiting for me with a glass of milk and a snack of cookies or fruit. She'd be planning dinner, or telling me to get in the car to come with her on some errand.

I first noticed it happening when I was around eight, and then at intervals that might be spaced out for months or sometimes years.

On one of my mother's 'bad' days, I would enter her room quietly, sit on the edge of her bed and tighten my insides into a solid core. She would pat my hair, and take my hand and stroke it. When I found her in bed, I knew I would need to be the one giving comfort.

"How was your day honey?"

"Fine, Mom. Are you sick?"

She would sit up, pull me toward her and hug me very hard. She'd whisper in my ear, "I love you so much sweetheart."

I would lean away. To distract her, I'd tell her how my friend Susie had to move to Kansas, and how we were all so sorry to see her go so far away. Did she think we should have a going away party for her? Or, I'd talk on and on about how much I wanted to learn to play *I Want to Hold Your Hand* on my guitar – anything to keep up the banter, to make her smile, to stay away from her pressing need for me.

I leaned away. I couldn't hold her together myself.

I was grateful when my father finally came home. He would take in the scene and immediately change his end-of-a-long-day tired face to the one he used to cheer up my mother.

"It's so nice out, I think I'll leave it out," he'd say with a wink at me. My mother would smile. Soon they would be talking about his day, about a customer who bought one of the new expensive digital watches. They'd laughed at the new silly watches, how people were so lazy these days they didn't even want to read a clock face anymore!

She would get up to make dinner, and I would sigh with relief.

Linda and I seemed to have different parents during our teenage years. To her, my mother was always critical – of her hair, her make-up, or whether she wore clothes that showed too much of her scarring. "She always wanted to fix something on me," Linda told me.

But their closeness showed in the way they fought with each other. She and my mother had knock down drag out fights all the time. It might be over clothes, or a boyfriend, or something trivial–but they did it wholeheartedly and with gusto. Usually there was yelling and slamming doors. It was thrilling. I watched from the sidelines, taking bets.

One of the big fights was when Linda dyed her hair blonde in high school. She naturally had beautiful thick jet-black hair. My mother hit the roof when she got home and saw what Linda had done. She screamed about Linda ruining her 'good asset,' that hadn't been taken by the fire, and Linda cried that all the girls were doing it. My mother blamed Linda's best friend for coercing her into the dye job and started going on about how the friend was no good and didn't care about Linda.

My mother and I had a more laissez-faire relationship. She was loving and sympathetic and usually tried to reason with me when we disagreed. She tried to coerce me with "Judy, do you think that's the best thing to do?" or "Judy, I really liked that other dress on you better" or, "Why don't you try a little eye make-up tonight?" If I disagreed, she would quickly throw up her hands and give in. I can't remember a time when we really fought. She might have gotten exasperated with me, especially when I couldn't make a decision, but she rarely yelled or slammed anything. I remember sometimes wishing she would, craving the kind of passionate connection she and my sister shared.

The mother I got, however, relied on me for emotional support, especially as I got older. I was the one she turned to when she was down, or had complaints about my father.

"Love doesn't last," she told me one day on the way to my guitar lesson when I was nine. "Just don't think it does. Money lasts."

My father was a completely different case. He was Linda's cheerleader and confidant.

Linda told me she used to wait until everyone else had gone to bed and my father would be in the kitchen reading, or having a snack, so that she could have alone time with him.

As far as my father was concerned, Linda was always perfect, and he forgave her almost anything if it could make her happy for even a moment. His theory was that she deserved it. She had been through so much, that anything she did to give herself a good day, he supported. He even told her as much. My father always came through with just the right compliment for Linda, and just the right joke to lighten her spirits when she needed it. I remember being glad she had that from him, and pushing down the feeling that I wanted some of it for myself.

The only time he got angry where Linda was concerned was when someone else tried to take advantage of her or hurt her. He bought off the greasy hood boyfriend Linda had as a teenager so he would leave her alone. I thought he would kill the boyfriend who asked Linda to marry him before he went to Viet Nam, but was actually engaged to another girl at the same time. My father was small, but wirey–and he owned a gun.

In contrast, when I was heartbroken over a boy when I was 16, my father treated it like a frivolous episode. I was face down, crying into my pillow when I heard my mother urging him to come to comfort me. I could almost hear him wince and shrug before he opened the door to my room. He sat on the edge of my bed and tentatively patted my back for a minute.

"Oh, come on Judy, you're so young, you don't want to get tied down with one boy right now," he said. "There'll be plenty of boys in the future for you."

I would cry even harder then, until he left.

Until the baseball to the nose incident, I was daddy's little girl, but after that there was some kind of break in the way he treated me as I entered adolescence. He resisted my becoming a young woman. He was the one, for instance, that I had to get permission from to shave my legs, which now seems totally absurd and inappropriate.

And, when he observed that it was time for me to stop running around the house without a shirt on, on hot summer nights, it was with a hint of disgust. I was morphing into a different animal, and he was not happy about it.

More than once, I overheard him tell my mother not to tell me I was pretty because it "would go to her head." I only got a nod and a smile even when I dressed up for my first junior prom, had my hair done for the first time, and wore a long frilly gown.

His indifference fed my growing dissatisfaction with myself and magnified my self-consciousness. As a result, I tied to blend in as much as possible with the woodwork. At 14 I grew my hair long, wore Army-Navy surplus jeans and jackets and wore no make-up to speak of. The effect was to become completely generic and nearly invisible. You could have exchanged me with any other teenager in town and not noticed the difference. On the other hand, I sought attention from any male that found me attractive. Not that I was promiscuous. I was too much of a late bloomer for that. But, in my mind and heart, my father made me a sucker for any boy that showed an interest. I was a psychological push over, and maybe even more vulnerable than I would have been if it were just my body I were giving away. Every unkind word or rejection from a target of affection would sear the delicate skin of my self-esteem. I switched boyfriends frequently so I wouldn't get too invested in one relationship. It was a hard habit to break.

Chapter Twenty-Five
2005

It's a cold, rainy winter day. A light fog is lifting in my back yard. The trunks of the trees look like they reach up forever, with the greenery obscured in the earth bound clouds. The very type of weather of the day of the crash, I think. The kind of day I am glad I'm not getting up at 6 am and traipsing out in the cold to go to an office. I'm happy to put on a pot of tea and settle in to work. Lately, my 'project' is taking more and more of my work time.

I'm not exactly sure what I'm looking for as I rifle through the material I brought home from the library. The headlines I find in the old newspaper clips still feel remote, like they are about any family, any tragedy. Even seeing the pictures of my parents and my sisters in the articles, I feel detached. It's not the connection I want. None of it offers any clues to how I fit into their survival or gives me an outline of my own portrait that I can begin to color in.

I'm beginning to wonder if this is all just a way for me to stay with them, to keep my parents in my life since their death. A friend warned me recently that writing about the recently dead is dangerous for them. It keeps them tethered to this life, not releasing them to the next. If that's true, I guess I have to apologize to my parents–but I cannot seem to stop myself.

I concentrate on information about the crash site, the ashes from which I eventually rose. When the smoke cleared, I learn that there was one engine of the plane embedded in a mass of wreckage 30 feet from my parents' home, and the nose of the aircraft was in the basement of the house next-door. The left wing tip rested in the back yard of a yellow frame house at 658 South Street. The belly of the plane sheared off the top of my parents' building and spewed fuel into my mother's kitchen in a burst of flame.

Some of the details fascinate me. Whether they help my search or not, I can't look away. Like the book found in the rubble of the crash – *Passage into Peril.* Or, learning that one semi-famous man, former Secretary of War Robert P. Patterson died in the plane.

Uncovering more, the impact of the crash seems to spiral out, like great ripples, or the famed butterfly effect. Each beat of the butterfly's wings affecting far-reaching weather patterns across the globe.

All tolled, 31 people died as a result of the crash, but that official death toll didn't include the miscarriage of Captain Reid's unborn child. I find an account written by one of Captain Reid's surviving daughters, who had done her own research about the crash that killed her father. *Something had gone terribly wrong with that plane,* she wrote. *In the autopsy, both his wrists were broken from struggling against the controls.* I want to contact her, a kindred survivor, but I have no idea how to find her.

The headlines following the accident give me only a tiny glimpse into what went on for my family in the aftermath of the crash. In the article **Hospital Treats Survivors**, from *The Elizabeth Daily Journal,* there is a photo of my mother lying in a hospital bed a day after the accident. Her vacant eyes, the knit of her brow, the rigid set of her mouth reflect the lost child, the near-death baby. I search her face for a hint of the woman I knew as my mother, but cannot ascertain the protective shell, the steely façade that may have germinated here in the flash of a camera. A photo next to this one shows little Linda in an oxygen tent. Mostly a bundle of bandages, with only a glimpse of her eyes. It's all a cartoon of tragedy. I wish I could put my hand over the photographer's lens and push him away.

CONDITION IMPROVES: Mrs. Florence Mandel, of 310 Williamson street, mother of Donna, plane victim, and Linda, badly burned in tragedy, is reported to be improving at St. Elizabeth Hospital where she has been recovering from burns and shock.

A glamour shot of my mother takes a quarter page under the headline: **Condition Improves**, from *The Newark Evening News*. It is an old photo – her before face. Her beautiful eyes sparkle even in grainy black and white. She glances over her shoulder playfully, like a starlet. The relaxed smile beckons the photographer. She is a different woman from the one in the other article, where her features were remarkably transformed.

In the article, **Separated in Death** from *The Elizabeth Star Ledger*, my two sisters are in a formal shot with the sensationalist headline, taken just weeks before the accident. Linda's unmarred face draws me and I realize how much her life changed in an instant. Donna is the confident big sister, lording over Linda protectively. Her maternal instincts, overly developed for her seven years, would be put to a definitive test very soon.

Chapter Twenty-Six
JANUARY 22, 1952
DAY OF THE CRASH
2:00 PM

Their afternoon ran late, but my mother knew that Donna and her friend Sheila planned to stay after school to work on a project, so she still had some time to clean up and bake some cookies. They weren't expected home until 4:30.

"Let's go upstairs and tell grandma we're home, sweetie," she told Linda. "Then I'll make those cookies I promised. You were such a good girl at the doctor. The girls will be here in a little while to practice the skit for the B'nai Brith show tonight at temple, and Donna will be home soon."

My mother could hear the Pagoulatos' upstairs bringing in some bags from the market.

When Captain Reid landed in Syracuse, he went into the American Airlines office to check the weather. He saw no problem with landing in Newark, he told them. The plane was fueled with 340 gallons, bringing the total amount of fuel to 900 gallons. Flight 6780 was carrying 20 passengers, 85 pounds of mail, 112 pounds of air express and 400 pounds of ballast. It took off from Syracuse at 2:01 pm.

Chapter Twenty-Seven
Enter Music
1963

"They look like ragamuffins," my father said, frowning, halfway through *I Want to Hold Your Hand* when we watched the new band from England on The Ed Sullivan Show. I was nine.

"Dad, what are beatles anyway?" I asked.

"They're like roaches. Pests! Fits 'em. These *meshuganas* are just a flash in the pan, they'll never last. They can't even comb their hair!"

But I was entranced. First by Paul McCartney, then by the sound. It started my love affair with music, the silken thread to connect me to something my father also loved. I begged him to buy me a guitar.

Months later, he brought one home – the one I'd pointed out each time we went to Woolworth's that was packaged in a cardboard box with a cellophane window, and marked $15.98. It had a mottled amber wood front with a black back and came with a red plastic pick, a black guitar strap and a songbook.

If I Had a Hammer was the first song I could play all the way through. I learned songs by Bob Dylan, Peter, Paul and Mary, and, of course, The Beatles. My mother found a small music store nearby where I had lessons once a week and I practiced every day after school. The steel strings cut through my soft fingertips until I built up calluses on my left hand.

My father would often be crooning *Moon River* while Linda played the organ in the living room, tipping his head up and closing his eyes when he hit a high note. She was nimble with the foot pedals, her legs strong now. Building them up from her leg operation was the reason we got the organ. I wanted a piano.

But now that I had the guitar, I started singing as I played and my father seemed to take an interest. One day as I played in my room, sitting on my bed, I heard my father say to my mother, "She's not half bad you know, maybe I should show her some things about singing." That was the first time I considered that I might have a talent all my own.

From then on I could count on my father showing up while I practiced. Leaning up against the doorframe of my bedroom for a few minutes at a time shouting advice as I sang.

"Always hold your notes on the vowel, not the consonant. No one wants to hear Mmmmmoon River."

I listened hard and tried to do what he said. He never came into the room, or sat down to sing with me. He was always on his way somewhere else in the house when he stopped by.

I never did learn to play *Moon River* or *The Impossible Dream*, so my father never sang with me. Linda and I couldn't figure out how to play together, either. I strummed the chords of a song, and she played the melody, but it never came out as music. So, when the family came over–the Aunts and Uncles and cousins–it was still just my father and Linda at the organ. I don't know why I never sang with them. It seemed a kind of intrusion on my father's singing style. Sometimes they'd ask me to play something for them on guitar. I was a solo act.

When I sang, though, it transported me. I was surgically removed.

My father thought I should record a "demo" record and took me to a music store in Newark that had a small recording studio in the back. This sounded to me like he knew the music business and, best of all, that he thought I had some talent.

When we got there, the manager of the store led me into a tiny booth and went back around behind a glass window with my father. The ceiling was plastered with foam rubber and the walls were lined with egg cartons. The guy behind the glass pointed to the headphones hanging on the wall and I put them on. I adjusted the microphone and took out my guitar, sure I'd be discovered any second.

I remembered that my father said we'd be charged by the minute, so I didn't dawdle. I tuned up quickly and started my song. My own voice reverberated in my head and the guitar sounded distant through the one microphone.

Miraculously, we walked out with a thick vinyl record and I wondered which record store would now sell it for us.

"What do we do with it now, Dad?" I asked.

"Well, let me talk to a few people I know and see what we can do. We'll see Juicy."

His belief in me that day is what I remember most. ●

My mother got me my first "gig" at a fund raiser. My big numbers were *What the World Needs Now* and *More.* Suddenly, I was the family star and I relished the shift in attention from Linda to me.

Rehearsing with my father for the show was the most time we ever spent together alone. For our rehearsals now, I would bring my guitar down to the living room, me on the couch and him on the chair facing me. He taught me to breathe right while I sang –"Not with your shoulders–from the diaphragm–your shoulders shouldn't move." How to hit the high notes: "Think about the note, hear it in your head and you'll reach it, relax your throat muscles."

And the all-important, "Look at your audience when you sing, make eye contact and smile."

My father was a featured act at our swim club each summer, singing his favorite songs from musicals: *Pajama Game; South Pacific.* My mother would be backstage, fixing costumes or troubleshooting a makeup crises. Linda and I were out front, cheering for our star.

The time he spent with me sharing his music and knowledge was something I cherished – a gift. It was just between us, like the old days when he would put aside time to play catch with me in the backyard. With music, I had found a common ground that didn't entail changing my gender. It was something we would share through the years.

Peaking out from behind the curtain, I could see the simple set up. Just the wooden stool and mike on the bare stage.

The school auditorium was full for the school talent show. I was in fifth grade, giving my first performance for a crowd, and I was nervous. I saw all my teachers, friends and neighbors out in the audience. Even Roy, the crossing guard, waved to me from the back of the room.

It had been noisy just a minute ago, after Doug's rock n' roll band performed, but when I walked on stage it got very quiet.

I went over to the stool and took the mike from Mrs. Steinhart, who whispered, "Don't worry honey, they'll love you!"

My heart pounded eighth notes as the audience applauded and I sat down. My parents and Linda were sitting in the second row. My father smiled and gave me a thumbs-up. Then he pointed to his own mouth, my cue to smile at the audience. My mother did not seem to be breathing.

I checked the tuning of my guitar one more time. My father's eyebrows crinkled.

"Tune it before you go out," he told me the night before. "It's so annoying when bands come out and tune up their instruments for a half hour."

But he didn't understand. If one of the strings was flat or sharp, it would throw me and I'd sing off key. So I checked and double checked, and avoided his disapproving gaze.

"This is a song called *Surgery* that I found in a book of very old folksongs. I'd like to dedicate this to all the future doctors here tonight," I said.

I got a few laughs at that line. My father thought it was very funny, but I was not so sure. He was tickled with the song itself and thought it was meant for one me to sing.

I played the first few chords, and started to relax, letting the music lift itself out of me, like it had been hiding there all along. It took me soaring in its updraft, propelling me to crescendo. Laying me out before the audience.

I played a measure and sang:

Surgery, surgery,
first you slice and then you stitch…
cut it out and you'll be rich.

The audience faded to a soft blur and my fingers found the chords automatically. My hours of practice paid off and I was totally immersed in the music. When I finished, there was a surprising amount of applause and they were actually standing up. The crowd held me tight, and I let them have me. I filled myself with them and floated away.

Chapter Twenty-Eight
2006

I feel caught between the past, the present and the future. Still collecting details on the crash, and working to understand my parents' lives, I'm trying to connect the dots to my own. I also need to stay grounded in my present life, trying to build my writing business and also planning for Justin's upcoming high school graduation. Lately, we are discussing a graduation party, which he is resisting. I am a celebrator, but my son keeps a low profile. "Everyone is having a party, Mom," he says. "No one will even want to come." I'm sure that's not remotely possible, since he has a great group of friends that are always around. We compromise and pick a weekend when no one else in his group has planned anything. A pool party in July sounds good, so we start putting together an invitation list and I start planning the food. The planning keeps me from thinking about this next phase of my life where being a mother is not front and center. People tell me I will get used to having my son away, but I can't imagine it.

I pull out a file of newspaper articles and start my day's research to find out more specifics of the crash, what the neighbors were doing, how many escaped, and who did not. Somehow, this information seems important.

I now know of the Rangones, who rented rooms from Rosa Caruso at #306 Williamson. Ann Rangone, and her two boys – Emil, three and Robert, just 18 months – were at home that afternoon, along with Rosa and her husband.

Then, there were Michael and Christina Pagoulato, who lived in the third floor apartment above my parents. Michael came to America from Greece as a young man, and fought in the American Army in WWI. After the war, he returned to Greece just long enough to meet his future wife. Michael and Christina had two sons, George and Thomas, who were studying at Trenton State College.

Karl Reuling, Jr., a substitute teacher at St. Mary's High School just down the street, rented a room with the Pagoulatos on the third floor. He kept his class late that day because they had misbehaved.

Next door, at #312 Williamson Street, Mary Kaspar was putting up some new wallpaper in her bedroom that afternoon. And, at #314, Mrs. Schwartz was babysitting for her four-month old nephew, feeding him a bottle while her own two children played with their tinker toys in the next room. Mrs. Fetske, who lived in the small converted machine shop about 40 feet behind my parents building, was on the second floor sewing. Her three children were in the next room changing their clothes after school.

Just before the crash, about a dozen kids walked from St. Mary's School to the candy shop below my family's apartment to drink sodas and play pinball.

Across the street, three hundred students were at Battin High in basketball practice, Debate Club, Drama Club and rehearsal for the senior class play.

At St. Elizabeth's Hospital, down the road, the nuns had just been briefed on their disaster plan. Director of Nurses, Sister Maria Lawrence, concluded the meeting saying, *We've already had one plane crash, prospects for another seem remote.*

As I unearth more facts about the crash, the story gets slippery. More to the point, I still can't pluck my own story from inside this larger one. The more I uncover, the more I disappear into the background.

Chapter Twenty-Nine
JANUARY 22, 1952
DAY OF THE CRASH
2:21 PM

Flight 6780 was over Cortland, New York, flying at 7,000 feet in accordance with the flight plan. It continued over Lake Carey, Pennsylvania and reported in over Branchville, New Jersey.

Chapter Thirty
1964

Lucy and Ethel were working at the candy factory, the candy conveyor belt moving at a moderate speed while they wrapped each candy in tissue paper. Then it sped up and Lucy started popping candies into her mouth, stuffing them in her hat and down the front of her dress. The supervisor came in and Lucy's candy-filled hat flopped over her eyes and Ethel's mouth overflowed with chocolate. As we watched our favorite *I Love Lucy* TV show, Linda and I doubled up laughing. I was ten, she was 15, and this was one of those timeless shows we could still laugh at together.

We didn't notice my mother standing behind the couch.

"Can you girls come up to the kitchen? Dad and I have something we need to talk to you about."

Linda and I exchanged confused looks and followed her upstairs. My father sat at the kitchen table and we took our usual dinner time seats – Linda in the corner by the wall, me on the side by the refrigerator. My mother stood behind my father's chair, the window of the built-in oven reflecting a halo around her.

"Girls," my father started, "I don't want you to worry, things will be fine, but I wanted to let you know that I'm closing up the store."

"It's just not making enough money, and I owe quite a bit. But that's not for you to concern yourselves. We'll get through this and be better than ever."

My mother put her hands lightly on his shoulders, "That's right, things are going to be fine. It will just take a little while." I could tell that my mother had orchestrated this conversation.

I didn't know then that the extra costs of Linda's surgeries had put a big strain on the family finances. It was my mother that saw the store was a losing proposition and convinced my father to stop putting good money after bad and to move on.

"Nothing is going to change really. We'll just have to tighten our belts for a little while. Then I'll get another job and we'll be back to normal, ok, Juicy?" my father said with a wink at me.

I wondered how making my belt tighter would help. But, I was convinced. My parents were all powerful.

Linda said nothing and folded her hands in front of her on top of the table. She may have been thinking about how they would afford college, which was around the corner for her.

It seemed to me that my father *was* Goldblatt Jewelers. He had owned it for nearly 15 years and before that, he worked for Mrs. Goldblatt. I couldn't imagine him apart from the store. His world revolved around the place where he built up clientele and friendships. He was there six-days-a-week, with Blue Laws giving him one day of rest on Sundays.

Sundays, I would follow him around like a puppy when I was little. Looking back, it was my mother that deposited me firmly under his jurisdiction on that day of the week. If he went bowling with his league, I would tag along. Or, if he was going to the hardware store to pick something up, my mother would tell him to bring me too.

When my father closed his store, the *Everything Must Go* sale turned into a reunion for all of his customers. It was just like the

Christmas rush when the whole family helped out in the store. Those are some of my happiest memories. I was the quarterback of the team and could wrap a package in a minute flat, or clean a tray of rings in no time. We arranged and re-arranged the displays as things were sold. At this last sale, my father said goodbye to lifelong friends, with everyone swearing to keep in touch.

In a photo of my father in front of his store on Broad Street, he wore a diamond tie bar just visible above his jacket buttons – "Easier to sell them when I'm wearing one." He posed proudly in front of his display window with the silver giftware polished by my mother, arranged by him.

After closing Goldblatt's, my father got a job as a manager with a large jewelry chain. And he was very successful there, winning awards and trips. It was the first time my parents had a chance to travel – to the Caribbean, to the company headquarters in Texas, meetings in LA, San Diego and San Francisco. These were the good times they talked about for years and remembered fondly in their eighties.

With the new job, calls from creditors stopped, and my mother started answering the phone again. She was calmer and my father cracked more jokes. We had barbecues and holiday dinners with aunts, uncles and cousins again.

After he died, I found a letter from the top executive of that jewelry chain, one of my father's prize possessions, in the strong box under his bed:

"Al is an exceptional manager. His knowledge and experience in the jewelry business are invaluable as our top salesman."

The letter was folded twice over and yellowed with age. It was the only document, other than his wishes for cremation, "like his little girl" held in the steel box.

Chapter Thirty-One **2006**

The auditorium is packed with people and I'm straining to find my son among all the blue gowns. The music has started, and the class is marching in from two doors on opposite sides of the room. I don't know where to look. It's also a little hard to see anything through the blur of water that has collected in my eyes. I didn't expect the rush of emotion today at his graduation. Part of it, I know, is wishing my parents could be here to see their grandson graduating with honors, tall and strong and handsome, with his warm smile and a kindness of spirit that is rare in teenagers. My mother saw it though, she could feel it in his hugs, she said. Another part is that I am so very proud of this boy and, still another is that I realize the biggest part of my mothering job is behind me. I'm not at all sure I always did the best for him. I'm haunted by something someone said to me when I was pregnant, that the best thing I could do for my baby was to stay together with his father. That was the one thing I couldn't do.

When I met Bob, Justin's dad, I was sure I had found my soul mate. He was sensitive and kind. We cried at movies together. He was caring when I was sick. I thought he was responsible and that I could trust him, since he was a bank manager when we met. In the beginning, he was attentive and affectionate, though that faded pretty quickly after we married. We also had a common bond of being married twice before, which was sometimes a stigma with other men I had met.

When we first dated, Bob took me to expensive restaurants nearly every night of the week and wowed me with gifts for birthdays and holidays. It wasn't until much later that I found out he cleaned out his savings and investments to finance that courtship.

When I brought him to Florida to meet my parents, we all got together with his father and stepmother who lived close by. The families hit it off and got along well. But when we got home, Bob got a call from his father almost immediately who warned him that if he didn't tell me the truth – he would tell me himself. The truth that I didn't know was that Bob was not divorced. Now that his father had met my parents, he said, he couldn't let him lie to me any longer. That led to a long process of obtaining the actual divorce, and proving to me and his father that it had been done by producing the final papers. Still later I learned that he had a daughter that he was not allowed to have any contact with. Yet, I ignored all the signs.

No, I couldn't stay with Justin's father. I only hope I made up for it with stability and love.

Now, while Justin is running all over town with friends, and working a part time job this last summer before college, I am being more and more overtaken by the past. I'm spending more time these days sifting through documents, and through my own memories.

I try to find someone or something to blame for the accident in the piles of notes and newspaper clips, but none reveals itself. Apparently, the plane was working just fine. The pilot was stellar. The reports all said the engines had no malfunction. The landing gear was down and both flaps were extended, and nothing else was found that failed structurally. Even the maintenance records for the plane showed it was in good shape.

It's possible that some birds flew into the plane, but they didn't find any bird remains in the engine parts.

From 26 witness statements, and The Civil Aeronautics Board Accident Investigation Report, I learn that the aircraft was flying at an altitude of 100-150 feet, just below the clouds, in a generally easterly direction, for a distance of about three city blocks before it went down. They all say it was flying level to the ground. Until it wasn't.

Witnesses heard: *Loud bangs, with a roar; Rumbling as it passed over; Sound of a car when all the spark plugs are not working; The noise stopped, the pilot speeded up motors as much as he could.*

My only hint is that the Investigation Report notes that carburetor icing could have been a factor. All but one of the pilots who landed just before and after the crash of #6780 said they used carburetor heat during their approach to avert icing. They didn't know if Captain Reid had used it or not.

The iffy weather seemed to affect only Flt #6780. During the two-hour period, one hour before and one hour after the crash, 19 flights landed or took off safely at Newark Airport.

Underneath the Civil Aeronautics Report, I find a faded newspaper clip of Linda celebrating her third birthday in the hospital. Surrounded by my mother and father, aunts, uncles and cousins. Linda is trying to smile. Her bottom eyelids are dragged toward her cheeks, her chin is soldered down to her little girl neck. Still, she smiles at the cake, the candles, her cousins standing with her. A defiant gleam in her eye.

NEWARK EVENING NEWS, MONDAY, JUNE 16, 1952

Hospital Party for Plane Victim

Little Linda Mandel marked her third birthday yesterday at St. Elizabeth Hospital, Elizabeth, where she is recovering from severe burns suffered in blaze that killed her sister Donna, 7, after plane crashed into their house at 31[illegible] Williamson street, Elizabeth, last January 22. Linda, daughter of Mr. and Mrs. Albert Mandel, who now live in Warinanco Village, Roselle, is visited here by relatives, Joyce Fischler of Elizabeth and Stuart Lipson of Cal[illegible]ia.

Chapter Thirty-Two
JANUARY 22, 1952
Day of the Crash
2:50 PM

Linden Suffel walked out of school with her friends to find her mother waiting for her in the car. She was on her way to my mother's apartment to rehearse for a skit at their temple that evening.

"The weather is so bad, I didn't want you walking to Mrs. Mandel's and coming home late in the dark. She'll understand. Just tell one of the girls to let her know," Mrs. Suffel told her daughter, and ushered her into the car.

Captain Reid was cleared by Air Traffic Control to maintain 7,000 feet over Branchville.

Chapter Thirty-Three
1966

By the time Linda was seventeen, she used special theatrical make-up designed to cover the red and brown raised scar tissue. It performed miracles for her, covering the scars and letting her features emerge like a painting.

I used to watch her sitting at her vanity table that my mother got her, artistically recreating herself one brush stroke at a time. There were jars and bottles of creams and powders, brushes, pencils, application pads and sponges filling the small plastic surface and tucked beneath a narrow shelf. Linda was adept at using the pink and green tints to counter the corresponding brown or red tones of the scars. Then, applying the paste-like foundation and a layer of white powder, she would set the base. The finishing touches transcended the sum of the parts; the hint of blush to the cheeks, the tasteful black outline of the eyes, the extension of lush lashes. It all came together with the delicate balance of a Renoir.

I marveled at how she knew just where to put what and at her skill, and patience. It would take her at least an hour to get the results she wanted. I knew from listening to my parents that the stuff was very expensive, so she was careful not to waste it when she wasn't going out. I'd heard my mother assure her that she would make sure she could always afford her makeup.

When I was around 14 and could have started wearing makeup, I totally dismissed the notion. Perhaps it was some kind of reaction, or rebellion, to seeing my sister chained to that vanity table for so many hours, so dependent on the transformation that the creams and powders provided. This was another source of Linda's resentment toward me. Me and my face could go anywhere right out of the shower. It was a daily affront and I figured I didn't need to make matters worse by adding eyeliner and blush. Even so, she used to accuse me of attracting boys whenever we went anywhere. "You don't have to do anything," she'd say. "They just seem to gravitate to you!" I did not agree with her that that was the case, but she generally persisted in pointing it out all through my adolescence so much so that I made a conscious effort not to even look at any boys when Linda and I were out together. I tried to blend into the background, make myself smaller, and dress in dark colors. I don't think I bought my first piece of makeup until I was 22.

When Linda was 17 and I was 12, a cosmetic surgeon offered to attempt to graft new skin to Linda's face–something no one had tried before. For the first time, she allowed herself to imagine her face without scars.

She dreamed and I dreamed with her. How would boys react to her with her new face? Would she be asked to the prom now? Could she put behind her the kind of rejection she experienced at those awful spin the bottle games in junior high? How might her world expand?

I wanted this for her as much as she wanted it for herself. It was a chance to even things out between us, and to maybe look like sisters – the chance to erase my unfair advantage.

Linda was buoyant about this hospital trip. It was the one surgery she had waited for, and that I ever remember her being excited about. I helped her pack her favorite nightgowns for the trip, like she was going on a honeymoon. She didn't pack any makeup.

Before she left that day, she gave me a tighter than usual squeeze, took a deep breath and a long hard look at me.

She was admitted overnight at Columbia Presbyterian in New York City, prepped for surgery the next morning, and put under anesthesia. When she woke up, however, the news wasn't good. My mother stood next to the doctor when he told her why she had no bandages, as she had expected.

"The scar tissue is just too close to the nerves to do this kind of surgery," the surgeon explained. "You could wind up much worse if we went ahead, with a possible paralysis of your face. I'm very sorry."

I can't imagine what my sister went through hearing this very final verdict. Later, she told me that was when she decided she was done trying to make herself over. She didn't want any more surgery to reconstruct, reconnect or realign anything anymore. My mother tried to convince her for a while to get more done, but Linda was adamant and refused.

Meanwhile, I had heard the news at home and waited on the curb outside our house anxiously for them to return. I thought they would have packed up and left the hospital right away, and should be home any minute. I wanted to hug my sister and tell her everything would be fine. By that time, my protective instincts for Linda were well-honed and I felt she would need me now.

"Hey Juicy, whatcha doin' out here," my father sat down next to me.

"Waiting for Linda and Mom. They're on their way home from the hospital, right?"

"Well, I just got off the phone with Mom. They aren't coming straight home. They decided to go to Washington, D.C. for a few days."

"What? We were all supposed to go there–together!"

We had talked as a family about making this trip to visit the monuments and the Smithsonian museums.

"It's to cheer Linda up, since they couldn't do this face surgery thing. They were all packed anyway, so Mom thought they would just get in the car and drive for a little getaway. This was very hard for your sister, Judy. I told her you would understand."

I tried to understand. I really did. It made perfect sense and I knew how disappointed Linda must have been that they couldn't fix the scars on her face. I was too.

"Yea, that's ok," I told my father then, trying to hide my disappointment.

But I felt like I was in a movie and the camera was zooming away, making me smaller and smaller – until I disappeared.

Chapter Thirty-Four
2006

I'm waiting for Justin to get home from school and fill the house with music. Even though I should keep working on some of my corporate writing that helps pay the bills, I look forward to the excuse to put it aside and talk to my boy. Or listen to him playing the piano, or even blare the music that we sometimes disagree on. Although, often I'm pleasantly surprised when he chooses to play some Bob Dylan or Grateful Dead.

My home office is plastered with the photos and the newspaper clips I've been piecing together. It's not yet a year since my mother passed away, and I find myself staring at her photo for a long time. I remember her mostly now as the woman I knew when I was a child. Beautiful, robust, fun loving and giving and I think of the things I should have done as her daughter, that I did not do, or did not think of doing. All the things I could have done for her at the end to make it easier.

I am also coming to grips with the reality of my father's life and the hole he left in mine. The more I relive our past together, the more I understand my own feelings toward him, as well as some of my own motivations throughout much of my life, especially in my choices of men. As much as my father was the comic, fun loving guy, I latched on to the defining nucleus of our relationship – a stoic distance.

Still, as I recreate that awful day and its aftermath, with the notes from my family and every scrap of detail from newspapers and investigative reports found on the Web, my own childhood fades to gray – as insignificant as it felt when I was going through it. How could anything in my life compare to what the rest of my family members had been through? To what they suffered, and what they lost? I am still a footnote in the story, stranded outside.

My most mundane episodes, along with the days that stand out in a bright white light, were infused with my parents' hopes and fears, their grief and loss. I was a sponge, thirstily soaking up the spillage of the tragedy.

I pick up a photo of me at age 13 at my Bat Mitzvah from the pile next to my desk. Linda and I both went to religious school and were part of the first generation of women to go through the coming of age ritual. It was meant to acknowledge us as equal partners before God and raise up our worth in our clan.

I studied for the ceremony for a year. The Hebrew was difficult, but once I got the melodies in my head it was just like learning new songs. *I Want to Hold Your Hand* in code. For me, it was a performance. My father listened to me practice, since he knew Hebrew.

Our learning Hebrew was important to my mother, especially since she never did. She often said to me, "I want my girls to be able to say the *Kaddish* for me after I die. I could never say it for my parents." She could never say it for Donna either.

My mother sewed remnants from my Bat Mitzvah dress to create a near-perfect mini-me on top of my celebration cake. The photo shows me sitting in front of the cake with my tiny twin perched on top of white icing, yellow roses at her feet, the navy blue background of our dress punctuated by white dots and outlined in yellow ribbon at the neck and hem. The yellow bow in my own hair matched the one on my replica on the cake. I imagined myself that perfect girl, morphing to womanhood on cue and committing to the God that saved one and let the other go.

My mother and I shopped for my dress for the ceremony, just the two of us, at Bambergers. My mother went there a lot, so she knew right where everything was. Junior girls on the second floor toward the back on the right, the tailored clothes I liked in one small section on the left.

The shopping trip was a sparring match. She found several dresses on the rack that she insisted, "would look so cute on you" and piled them on her arm for me to try. We lugged two armfuls of clothes into the dressing room. Once I had my clothes off, I was her prisoner and she brought me all the dresses she liked best.

She waited outside as I tried them on. I pulled the curtain closed behind me, the rings on top of the flimsy drape clinked like coins across the metal bar. Safely inside alone, I shrugged at myself in the mirror.

"Come out and show me what you put on," she begged me.

With Linda, it was different. My mother focused on finding her just the right dress, just the right skirt or blouse that coincided with all the rules around her clothes. Nothing sleeveless showing the tight red scarring on her upper arms. No low necklines revealing the scars on her neck and chest. Longer skirts to cover the scars on her legs.

On shopping trips with Linda, I'd go in a dressing room across the hallway to try on something and come out wearing it for my mother to see.

"Judy, just a minute, your sister is trying on this dress. I'll be right there."

"It's easy for you. You look good in everything," Linda would say.

My parents invited every relative to the party at our house after the services that I led at temple as part of the ceremony. We opened up the French doors onto the patio to fit them all. All the relatives remembered the accident, and this party was like a celebration of the survival of our family. My Bat Mitzvah seemed like a bargaining chip with God for my protection.

The party had a carnival feel. A kind of wild abandon. Aunts and uncles pinched my cheeks red.

Linda's Bat Mitzvah had been different. That day, I remember the hugs were deep and tears on the verge of spilling. Whiffs of memories from a time they didn't think Linda would make it to her third birthday, let alone this milestone.

Back in my office now, digging underneath the stack of photos, I find one that my mother carried with her of Justin at his Bar Mitzvah in 2000. My parents and Linda, her husband and her daughter, had been able to take the trip from Florida to Connecticut for his ceremony. The continuity of our family was in sharp relief that day. It all seemed a miracle that any of us was there.

Justin performed his part of the service flawlessly, and made us all very proud. I stood for photos with him and his father, and then with my husband and his three boys as well. Justin dutifully danced the first dance with me, the top of his head only reaching my shoulders. I recognized a heady lightness, *kveled* with pride and love, and thanked our God for this borrowed life.

My father was visibly moved when he handed down his well-worn tallis to Justin, the first male child in our family. Birthing a boy was one of my few achievements that solicited praise from my father.

Now, I am blasted out of my memories by Justin bursting into the house and pouncing on the piano to practice for his gig this weekend. He's playing one of my favorites: *Someday, My Prince Will Come.*

Chapter Thirty-Five
JANUARY 22, 1952
DAY OF THE CRASH
3:00 PM

Selma Kurtzer, Beverly Chessler and Leona Lewis rang my mother's doorbell. They had signed up at Temple Beth El to be in the skit that my mother was organizing for that night's event.

"Come on in girls!"

"Linden couldn't come–her mom wanted her to go straight home," Selma told my mother while they took off their wet coats.

"Well, I don't blame her in this weather. I think we should make it a quick rehearsal. The weather is so bad, you should get home before it starts getting dark."

"We've got the music you wanted, Mrs. Mandel," Leona said and handed her the sheet music.

She took out a pitch pipe to help them practice, since there was no piano at the apartment.

"Ok, girls, I'll give you a 'c' and you take it from there."

At School 19, Donna looked out the window.

"Why don't we finish up the project at my house–you can come over," Donna said to her friend Sheila. "It's so yucky out, I don't want to walk home in the dark."

Sheila agreed and they headed for home.

Chapter Thirty-Six 1967

I absolutely had to get out of that house. They still treated me like a kid even though I was 13. So, one Sunday I begged my father to buy *The New York Times* and look through the summer camp section with me. The sleepover section. My plan was to offer up my life's savings, saved from birthday presents, to pay for it.

I wanted a music and theater camp, to have a chance to be in a real production. Mostly, to be somewhere I could be just me, and not my mother's daughter. Or my sister's sister.

Somehow, I talked my parents into letting me go to the camp sight unseen. My duffle bag was packed with everything on the camp list: four pairs of shorts; two bathing suits; six pairs of socks; sneakers; sandals; four T-shirts; a pair of jeans; towels and toiletries. It was my first trip away from home. I was excited, but also a little scared on the four-hour drive up to Camp Tomoka in Becket, Massachusetts.

To be able to truly recreate myself at camp, I didn't tell anyone about my family tragedy. I would leave the dead sister, the hurt sister, behind. They didn't need to know, and I could be seen without that excess baggage coloring their definition of me. There would be no sympathy –which I didn't feel I deserved – and no questions about Linda. This was my first experiment with being just Judy. It was a way of passing for a regular person.

It also felt like my first big adventure. I'd be out on my own with no one to tell me when to brush my teeth or make my bed and no one to point out every danger that might be lurking if I took a hike or a boat ride.

When we got there, I was shocked at the old house where I'd be sleeping. It was not the rustic log cabin in the woods in the ad, but a run-down old gray colonial in need of a paint job. A few shingles were missing on the roof, and some slats of siding were hanging at angles on the side of the house. There were six of us girls in a room, in bunk beds, with one shared bathroom.

And bugs. Nobody mentioned bugs. Caterpillars, ants, spiders. I planned to sleep in my clothes all summer.

We were told that all of us were expected to clean the place every day as part of our activities. I didn't count on scrubbing floors that summer. I sent my parents a letter telling them to pick me up, but when I hadn't heard from them three days later, I ran away.

The vast green open space of the countryside made me dizzy. I aimed for the main road we came in on. Surely there would be a town. After walking about a mile, I came to a combination store and Post Office that had a pay phone outside that promised freedom. I scrounged in my pocket for my leather money pouch with a few dollars of change.

When I got through to my mother, I was indignant. Didn't she get my letter? Didn't she know how awful this place was? Weren't they coming to get me?

"Why don't you give it a little time sweetheart," my mother said softly. "You just got there. Maybe you'll get used to it. It might be fun if you stick it out."

I hung up in disbelief. Abandoned. Alone. Desolate. I walked slowly back to camp. Resigned to my fate, I got into the routine, made some friends, and even landed the lead in the musical. I was one of the better singers that session. By the end of the first week I was having a great time and had to admit, as much as I hated to, that my mother was right.

I met my first real boyfriend that summer. Dean was a counselor at the boys' camp across the lake that came over on weekends for bonfires, singing, marshmallows and popcorn. I was sitting on the ground near the fire when he sat down next to me, pushing aside another boy that was cozying up to me.

"What's your name?"

I told him.

"Do you like it here?"

"Kind of," I said. I liked it more already.

Dean had the most soulful brown eyes I'd ever seen, and when he looked at me I felt recreated. He was 16 to my 13 and seemed very worldly, funny and smart. But what struck me most was that he liked me. It was unbelievable to me, and it turned out that was the only aphrodisiac I needed.

"What brings you to this camp?" he asked me. He handed me the marshmallow he had melted on a branch in the fire, a simple gesture that signaled his interest in me to the other boys around the fire. His attention made me feel important.

"I sing."

"That's cool. Lots of the girls here are dancers, going over to Jacob's Pillow for classes. I don't understand dancers."

"Me neither. It seems so hard, so much work. And they have lots of pains after they practice. I am not into pain."

He laughed. I made him laugh.

It was a challenge to hear our conversation above the fireside songs, and Dean grabbed my hand and motioned for me to follow him to a clearing away from the bonfire and the crowd. He put his arm around me. I began to feel almost beautiful.

"There, now we can hear each other," he said.

Dean told me he was there for his last summer as a counselor. Next year he'd get a real job. He went to a prep school in Scarsdale. He told me all about himself, but I couldn't really concentrate on his words with his arm around me. My stomach fluttered each time he smiled. It was a new sensation for me and I was nearly drunk on it.

He didn't snicker, or even smirk when I told him I wanted to be an actress and a singer.

When the counselors said to pack it in for the night, Dean and I had only just begun to get to know each other.

"Can you get out tonight?" he whispered.

"I have no idea. What do you mean?"

"In an hour. Sneak out of your room and meet me by that oak tree at the top of the hill over there."

"Really?"

"I don't want to let you go yet."

No one had ever said anything remotely like that to me before, and I wanted more. When I got back to my room and told my bunkmate, she said, "You have to go! I'll help you."

So after lights out, she helped me stuff my blanket and use one girl's wig to make it look like I was in the bed when they came around to count heads. I snuck down the stairs with my shoes in my hand and out to the oak tree.

Dean was waiting with a blanket spread out on the grass under the tree. It was a clear, cool, New England summer evening. The stars were in collusion with his plan, softly lighting our rendezvous. We talked for a while before Dean pulled me toward him and kissed me – the most kissing I'd ever done before. I tried to be nonchalant, like it was just another day in my glamorous life, but my heart was racing when I ran back to my room.

That summer I found a new confidence in being Dean's girl. It was the start of my looking to define my self through men that saw something special in me.

Chapter Thirty-Seven
1968

In Junior High, when kids in my class were going steady for a week at a time and then moving on to the next, I collected I.D. bracelets from anyone that gave me a second look. Some of my girlfriends were more discerning and chose their steady guys with much more thought; some even passed on an invitation. I could never do that. I always felt that if I refused, it might be my very last chance. This, after 10 or 12 boyfriends over a few months. Gratefully, going steady in seventh grade back then mostly entailed walking home from school together, letting the boy carry your books, and maybe some tentative closed-mouth kissing. Occasionally, there would be a school dance where you were expected to dance the slow dances with your steady. But by the end of the night, I had usually switched boyfriends anyway. The strobe lights and loud music made it surreal. Your life could change at one of those dances.

Music had also become a way for me to infiltrate the male dominated garage band scene. There was only room for one girl singer in a band, even if I was grudgingly included to sing the Jefferson Airplane or Janis Joplin tunes they wanted to play. I liked being the only girl in the room at rehearsals. I could imitate Grace Slick pretty well, but the growl of Janis was something that eluded me–and got me kicked out of a few groups.

In high school I finagled my way into the band with the lead singer I had a crush on. I'd seen him in a play at school and was instantly in love. His band played lots of Crosby, Stills and Nash tunes and I knew I could help them out on the harmonies. But really it was Ray I was after. He was a senior and I was a freshman, but I didn't think that should matter. He looked like a scruffy Robert Redford, with red-blonde shaggy hair and a drooping mustache that tickled when we kissed.

Going out with him was a big topic in our house. My parents went ballistic the first time Ray pulled up in his bright yellow VW van with its white roof. My father shook his head and muttered, my mother worried her eyebrows into one big wrinkle. But when Ray came in and met them, he was very charming. I was just glad they didn't look into the back of his van; Ray had taken all the seats out and put in a big mattress.

Ray was very much a gentleman with me. No one would have believed it to look at him, or his van, but he always stopped short of getting really physical with me. He kept telling me I was too young, and when things would heat up, he would distract me with one of our philosophical discussions about whether the Beatles or Rolling Stones were the fathers of modern rock 'n roll. I knew nothing at all about sex, or even the preliminaries. If Ray had pressed me at all, I probably would have done anything to keep him around telling me how pretty and talented I was. Later though, I learned that he was sleeping with one of my friends the whole time we were seeing each other.

One late afternoon, coming back from rehearsal and a little bit of a party, Ray and I pulled up to my house to find chaos. Two police cars flashed red over my front yard, the sound of their radios crackling.

"Oh my God! The cops are here!" was all I could register in my brain as Ray pulled the van into the driveway. I sat paralyzed, thinking something had happened to my parents or Linda while I was out partying.

"Let me just pull myself together before I get out," I told Ray. I realized I was looking a little too disheveled to face my parents and the police. I'd have to try to get into the bathroom and brush my teeth, splash my face and find something to cover the smell of the grass we'd been smoking.

But, Linda was running toward us, barefoot. She was never barefoot. She looked a mess, with her hair flying and her shirt hanging out of her pants.

"Where the hell have you been? We got a call that said it was you, and you had been hit by a car. Did you call?"

"What the hell are you talking about? I'm right here!"

"Well, you better go in and explain where you were. We couldn't find you anywhere. Mom and Dad are frantic." She gave Ray a dirty look.

"Just let me get into the bathroom first, ok? Before I have to talk to anyone."

"Ok, I'll cover for you."

It turned out it was a crank call. My mother couldn't remember if they even said my name–just that it sounded like me. It was probably her imagination. Imagining the worst that could happen, as usual. Me, lying in a ditch bleeding, miraculously crawling to a pay phone, finding a dime to call her one last time before collapsing into a coma. The dangerous, random world sucking me in to a black hole.

Chapter Thirty-Eight
2006

I'm trying to get organized. My office is a mess of newspapers, index cards and photos. There have been various methods I've tried over the last year to do this. File folders, file boxes, a special binding system that lets you pull out pages and replace them easily. None has worked for me. Now, I'm trying my old method of using notebooks. For the news clips, I'm using clear page protectors. So, now comes the task of filtering through the stuff for the umpteenth time. Each time, though, I've found another nugget that has sparked a feeling, a story, or a memory.

I find a headline that stops me cold, from *The Elizabeth Daily Journal,* January 24th, 1952 – two days after the crash: ***Funeral Rights Held for Mandel Girl.***

The date of the article makes me realize that my mother would not have been able to attend her daughter's funeral. She would have still been in the hospital recovering from her injuries. The burial could not be postponed, since Jewish law requires burial within 24 hours of death. Missing her last chance to say goodbye was undoubtedly one of many obstacles to my mother's grieving process that may have explained why she never fully healed, if healing is even possible from the death of your child.

My mother was denied all of the usual paths to coping with grief. There was no way to go back to Donna's room, reduced to ash, to look through her things and remember. No photos survived as a record of their life together, until they could later gather some from relatives.

Added to this, cremation is not recognized as a legitimate method of burial in the Jewish religion, though there was no choice where Donna was concerned.

Arrangements for Donna's funeral, I knew, were entirely in my father's hands. He would have had only a day to find a plot, a pine box according to Jewish tradition, and to secure the rabbi. He managed it all mechanically, like a sleepwalker.

The morning of the funeral, I imagine my father went to the hospital with the rabbi to have the Keria ribbons pinned on both he and my mother. He would have taken her bandaged hand lightly in his as the rabbi said a short prayer and pinned them both with the black frayed ribbon. I can envision him leaning carefully over the bed and kissing my mother, their tears mingling.

The scene takes shape in my mind. On the winding narrow road to the gravesite, the line of dark cars split the white-on-gray landscape. Tires smacked against wet tarmack. Only the whip-suck-whip of windshield wipers broke the leaden quiet.

The single plot nestled against a large oak tree, purchased in haste, was surrounded by deceased strangers, with no other Mandels nearby. My father told me the thought had never crossed his mind to buy cemetery plots for his young family.

Teachers and parents from Donna's school came to pay tribute at the funeral. Many neighbors, some who escaped the crash, or ran from the flames, were there: Girls from Battin High; Karl Reuling Jr. who lived upstairs; the St. Mary's kids from the candy store; Jack and Florence Earlman, whose daughter Sheila was still in intensive care.

Some officials were there, including the Elizabeth Mayor, the Chief of the Fire Department and the principal of Woodrow Wilson School.

It was unreal, unbelievable to my father that his precious girl was gone. Acting purely on autopilot, he was barely able to put one foot in front of the other and felt lost without my mother by his side.

The gathering at the grave was respectfully silent as the Rabbi read passages in English and Hebrew. They joined him in saying the *Kaddish*, but my father would not have recited the part of the *Kaddish* that translates to *blessed is the righteous judge*. For him, this would have been a lie. He never saw the senseless death of his baby girl as anything righteous. In fact, his faith was shaken to its core.

I follow my vision of the day through. As Donna's pine box was lowered into the ground, my father made no attempt to wipe away his tears. His sisters, Sylvia and Ruth, flanked him and each took an arm. He was the first to place a stone on the gravesite–Jewish tradition to leave behind a marker to show the deceased is not forgotten by family and friends.

Most of the crowd then made their way to their cars, but my father's sisters stayed with him until the last shovel of dirt was tapped down.

Afterwards, the family gathered at my Aunt Sylvia's house. Each person stopped to wash their hands from the pitcher of water at the doorway to purify themselves after close proximity to the dead. Inside, mirrors were covered with black cloth.

My father knew he couldn't be away from my mother and Linda during the entire Shiva period. At the end of the day, he found a bit of dirt from the garden outside Sylvia's home and placed it inside his shoe, so as not to forget his mourning state, and returned to the hospital.

Now, I put aside the news clip that placed me so squarely at my sister's funeral.

Chapter Thirty-Nine
JANUARY 22, 1952
DAY OF THE CRASH
3:21 PM

Flight 6780 was over Patterson, New Jersey. The plane was expected to land at 3:40 pm in Newark, where the weather was still foggy with a light rain and visibility of three quarters of a mile. In Elizabeth, my family's schedule was being adjusted by the cold, rainy day.

Chapter Forty 1964 - 1972

The five years between Linda and I were a chasm from the ages of 10 to 20.

In her high school years, from around 15 to 18, Linda chose a rougher group of friends than my parents would have liked. She started smoking and bleaching her hair. I was too young to know what else might have been happening, but I often heard the worried conversations through my parents' bedroom wall whenever Linda stayed out too late, or had a date with a boy my parents didn't like.

"We can't run her life for her, Al," my mother would say.

"But, that guy is just no good, I can tell. There must be some reason he keeps hanging around," my father would counter.

They never watched me as carefully, or were as invested in my daily life. I was pretty much a free agent.

When I was old enough, around 17, and she was young enough, about 22, we joined forces at times, plotting together to break away from the confining walls of our safe life. I'm sure now that, even though we didn't discuss it, we were both experimenting with sex as the validation we sought from boys, if for different reasons.

One weekend when my parents were away and Linda was home from college and left in charge, she conspired with me to have a forbidden party.

Before the guests arrived, she bought vodka and began to pour most of the bottle of Smirnoff into our punch bowl. "Don't put too much in there," I told her.

"Oh, you won't even taste it," she promised. We emptied containers of orange juice and cranberry juice into the bowl, then added four trays of ice.

I told 10 friends about the party, but when word got around town, the cars just kept coming. Pretty soon, there were kids all over the house I didn't recognize. Of course, after a few glasses of punch I didn't really notice.

We had the stereo turned all the way up. CSN&Y, "Our house is a very, very, very fine house…" and Rod Stewart wailing "spread your wings and let me come inside…"

When the party really started to get going, Linda left with her girlfriend for their own party at a friend's house.

Just then, my boyfriend Mike pulled up in his blue mustang convertible, threw his car door closed, his metallic black hair sweeping into his eyes. Since football season ended, he'd grown it nearly to his shoulders. He had on the beige shirt that hugged his chest, showing off his workouts.

Mike was a Junior to my Senior status and I'd be going off to college in a few months. He was the first boy I was serious about, and really cared for and I didn't want to lose him. So, we talked about it, and that night was indeed the night. I didn't have a burning desire to have sex, just the need for this boy to prove to me that I could be attractive and wanted. Mostly, I wanted to keep him around and waiting for me while I was away.

I had on my new denim halter-top, hip hugger bell-bottoms and a wide leather belt engraved with daisies and held with a chunky brass buckle. No jewelry, no shoes. My hair was straight and loose down my back.

Mike grabbed my bare waist and kissed me, slid his hand inside the back of my halter.

"Punch?" I offered.

"Sure," he took a gulp of the fruity stuff.

I swigged down the rest of my cup and took hold of his hand.

Gently touching my cheek, Mike turned my face to him, looked me in the eye, "Are you sure about this?"

Nodding a 'yes', I led him up the stairs to my room. I had drunk three plastic liter cups of the vodka juice, more liquor than the total I had ever consumed. I couldn't feel my feet hit the floor.

When we got to my room, I locked the door. The noise from the party downstairs faded and I could imagine we were alone. My idea of this moment was scripted by the movies. *Romeo and Juliet, Love Story, Bonnie and Clyde.* A confounding mix of images and non-information. What exactly do you do? Sex ed class only told us what *not* to do. I wanted romance, violins, the scent of roses.

I was pretty sure that I should not undress myself, but I didn't have to worry about that for long. We started kissing and Mike had me out of my top in about three seconds. Somehow, the rest of my clothes came off. "This will be great, you'll see," he said.

I unbuttoned Mike's shirt methodically down his chest like I'd seen Jane Fonda do with Robert Redford in *Barefoot in the Park.* Mike fumbled with his own pants, shoes and socks – no movie covered that – while I scurried under the covers, shivering.

When he held me, I caught my breath at the feel of his skin, the hard tightness of him against me, the smell of Brut cologne. I could have stopped there and been satisfied – or possibly passed out cold.

Mike held me still to calm me. He lifted my face to his, surprising me with his tenderness. Kissing first my eyes, my cheek and then grazing each lip separately. He had watched his own movies. The haze of vodka let me get lost in his kisses as his hands tripped down my sides, breasts and thighs, igniting new sensations. Still, my head was too blurry to register any ultimate pleasure. When Mike rolled on top of me I was mostly confused. And, then, quickly, it was over.

"Is that it?" I asked him after.

"It gets better," he said.

Before my parents got home on Sunday, I had scoured the house of any remnant of the party. Nevertheless, I missed something.

"Gidget, what is that you have in your mouth," I heard my mother say to our French poodle.

I could hear them through my bedroom wall.

"Al, look at this!"

I stood completely still to hear.

Whispers. Foot stomping down the stairs to the living room.

"JUDY, COME DOWN HERE!" My father yelled. "NOW!"

I tiptoed in, trying to assess the situation by their faces. It was not good.

"Sit!"

Gidget and I both sat.

My father threw a red square metal packet on the coffee table. My mouth fell open, saliva dried in my throat, sweat dampened my neck.

"It's a condom," he confirmed.

Gidget nosed under my hand, seeking forgiveness.

"So it is," I ventured.

"It's not our brand," my mother said.

I was shocked. I couldn't fathom why they would need condoms, never mind having their own brand, but I was relieved I could be somewhat truthful when I said, "I don't know where that came from." It wasn't the brand I used either.

My mother arched her right eyebrow and lowered her left. My father's upper lip disappeared into his lower one.

"Well, can you explain it then?"

"It must be Eileen's. I'm sorry, but I let her and her boyfriend use your room the other night when you were away."

This was absolutely true too. I used my own room.

"Oh my God!" My mother walked out of the room.

"See Flurry, I knew there would be an explanation," my father said calmly.

Chapter Forty-One 2006

All summer we've been getting ready for Justin to go off to college, planning what he'll need for his dorm room and what clothes he'll have to pack. Today we are taking him up to school in New York, to Sarah Lawrence College. It's a complicated affair to move him in. Justin's father and his girlfriend will follow David and I up there to see him off. Bob and I get along well enough, although our interactions are awkward and I'm afraid we'll both be vying to set up Justin's room and make his bed up. I'm fighting the feeling that this is my boy alone and I vow to make the day as easy as I can.

While he's packing I reason that it might be easier to concentrate on the past than the present so I find the folder with my mother's notes and bring it out to the porch where I can look out on the backyard. The trees and grass out there are still summer green.

For many years, my mother clipped news articles of larger settlements for what she deemed less devastating accidents or injury and her file folder is stuffed full of them. It didn't seem to matter if the cases held any similarity to theirs or not.

My mother's notes about the court settlement with the airline are specific, and Linda and my father also fleshed out the details for me about how the court case went.

Sometime in 1953, when Linda was well enough to go to court with them, their case against American Airlines was called. She was three.

My parents had spoken with their attorney and showed him the bills from the hospital. They explained the situation, and why it was imperative that they settle the case against American Airlines quickly, but with enough funds for the care Linda would need in the months and years ahead.

Like most people of that time, they had no health insurance, but skin grafts couldn't wait and the hospital had notified them that Linda could not receive any more care until the current bill was paid. The initial bill was staggering – over $5,000. More than my father made in a year then.

"Wouldn't it be better if we had a real trial–with a jury?" my father had asked the lawyer. "Wouldn't their sympathy help us?"

"Possibly, but that would take months more. I don't think you want to postpone Linda's care that long, do you?"

The family followed their attorney into the cavernous quiet of the Union County courtroom, a hush falling as Linda walked in ahead of her parents.

Four dapper young attorneys from the airline aimed their battalion of matching black leather portfolios at the judge. My father tucked his cardboard file under his seat.

In the middle of his opening remarks, without warning, the attorney picked Linda up under her arms and stood her up on the wooden table at the front of the courtroom. Linda remembers that she looked to my mother, and my mother grasped her hand. Meanwhile, the attorney was talking fast, pointing to the scars on Linda's arms and legs, pulling back her hair to reveal her missing ears, lifting up her sleeves and the hem of her dress to show the judge the extent of her injuries.

My father sat helpless, unable to stop the hurt in Linda's eyes.

After showcasing Linda's injuries, the attorney talked about the extent of the medical care she would need. He related the essence of the New Jersey aviation statute that held that *the owner of aircraft operated over land or waters of the state is absolutely liable for injuries to persons or property on land or water beneath, caused by ascent, descent, or flight of aircraft.*

He submitted photos of Donna and Linda before the plane crash.

Predictably, the defense noted that the Civil Aeronautics investigation was inconclusive: nothing was found wrong with the navigational gear or landing equipment; everything was functioning correctly. Captain Reid, too, was cleared of any negligence, and the criminal investigation turned up no determination of wrongdoing from the airline.

Their argument went a long way in reducing the financial award to $250,000. After attorney fees, the net to the family was $125,000.

Wrongful death awards typically take into account the potential earning power of the deceased for the family. So, the earning power of a seven-year-old didn't amount to much.

"It's still a lot of money," their attorney told them. "It should be plenty to take care of Linda. You'll see the money very quickly now, and it will all be settled."

In fact, the award was in line with others of the time. Some wrongful death suits yielded under $150,000. Catastrophic injuries could come in under $50,000. The $250,000 award was the equivalent of about $2 million in today's money.

Of course, the settlement didn't account for inflation, or medical expenses over Linda's lifetime. In the long run, it was not even close to enough, since the care she needed extended throughout her life.

The settlement was a hard kernel of resentment between my parents. My mother blamed my father for settling too quickly, and not choosing the right lawyer. My father would say nothing when she brought it up time and again. He would just walk away.

I urged her many times to let it go, give up on this particular frustration.

The car is jam packed with Justin's stuff: his electric piano and amp, his laptop and speakers, bedding and towels, clothes stuffed into duffle bags and plastic garbage bags, a couple of milk crates full of books. He is a big reader, and says he "needs" his books with him. I smile when I hear that. But taking all this with him looks like he will never need to come home again, and I already feel myself tearing up. I fight the urge and keep moving to get us on the road.

The day goes pretty smoothly. We find his dorm and battle the crowds of parents moving their freshman into their rooms. His roommates seem nice enough, although it is cramped for three boys in the one room. At the orientation session they firmly tell the parents to leave at 5 pm. The rest of the evening is for the students.

I try to make quick work of saying goodbye, and pull away from Justin's hug before I know I'll break down. He looks confused, and I give him another quick hug and tell him to call me soon. I get in my car and try not to look back. When I do look back, he has gone inside.

David and I have driven up in separate cars since there was so much to bring along, but we stay in contact on our cell phones. After we find our way to the highway, I call him and tell him I need to stop. He can tell I'm already crying and asks me if I'm ok. When we find a strip mall just off the road, I pull over and give in to my tears. David climbs into my car and leans over to hug me. Letting go of my little boy is harder than I ever imagined.

Chapter Forty-Two
JANUARY 22, 1952
DAY OF THE CRASH
3:37 PM

"Ok, I think that's enough practice–you will all do fine tonight," my mother told the girls. "Why don't you start for home, and I'll get ready for Donna to come home."

The girls gathered their belongings and left the apartment.

At the mention of her big sister, Linda was perched at the window. It was the highlight of her day, only trumped by my father's arrival at dinnertime.

"Donna, Donna!" Linda pointed down the block. A moment later, Donna and Sheila were clumping noisily up the steep stairs to the apartment, chatting and shedding their heavy coats. Donna was careful to lock the door behind her as she had been taught.

My mother looked at her watch. Donna was home a full hour earlier than expected.

Chapter Forty-Three
1967 – 1972

When I was in high school, Linda was away at college. My life was filled with a new sort of drama; a flurry of boyfriends, finding the right bell-bottom jeans and Pea jacket to keep up with my girlfriends, ironing my hair without burning it, and trying to stay out of the serious trouble some kids were getting into with drugs and sex.

One friend of mine was pregnant at 16, and another had such a bad acid trip that he was never the same. There were a couple of car accidents, related to driving under some influence or other. I realized that some of my parents' fears were, in fact, well founded. It was a time of such upheaval, I felt like my parents were from a different planet, not just a different generation.

I kept most of this kind of information firmly away from my parents. They were already so fearful that I was worried if I shared any of what was really going on at school and with friends, they might never let me out of the house again. Whereas they had always tried to protect me from the truth of their own tragedy, now it was my turn to protect them from the truth of my reality as a teenager growing up in the 60's.

It seemed some kind of miracle that they let me do half of the things I talked them into. Like going to Woodstock in '69, even though we got turned away and never made it into the festival. Or going with a friend to the May Day demonstration against the Viet Nam war in 1970 when we brought our sleeping bags and slept in the park by the Washington Monument. But my rebellion was mild in comparison with some. I didn't run to Haight Ashbury or do drugs. My crowd experimented with Harvey Wallbangers at one friend's house, and a little grass when it came our way.

At the same time, Linda was at Patterson State College majoring in speech pathology. She drove a white Dodge Dart convertible with red racing stripes along the sides. She had a small, tight knit group of girlfriends who were always going somewhere–the beach, a concert, a dance. She seemed to find her niche at school and I didn't need to worry about her.

She met Phil at a college dance. They had danced together all night, and he called her the next day, not knowing her name, but having gotten her number.

"You had the red dress on last night, right?" he confirmed when he reached her at her dorm. That was all he said he remembered.

An engineering student at a nearby school, Phil was a handsome boy with a kind smile and gentle eyes. He was very quiet, and somewhat shy, but he folded himself into our family quickly and completely. What I most liked about Phil was that he seemed to be able to do what we all did in the family – see through Linda's scars.

Just as we did, he didn't treat her any differently than anyone else. And, Linda seemed to be herself around him.

They married after they both graduated from college. Linda wanted to work with children, when speech therapy is most needed, but she was turned down for job after job because people thought she would frighten the kids. I always thought they overlooked how accepting children can be when they have an explanation. Mostly, they just want to know what happened. In any case, no school or hospital would give her a chance at the profession she had studied.

For a while, Linda had a fairy tale life as far as I knew. Phil landed a good job and they bought a house in the suburbs in New Jersey. They had two beautiful daughters, Cheryl and Debbie. The babies were another "miracle" – the doctors had said she could never conceive because of her extensive radiation exposure from X-rays over the years.

I was surprised when the marriage ended. All I know is that they tried marriage counseling, which didn't work. Linda moved back home for a little while after that, then to an apartment near my parents. She worked at a hospital in medical records for several years before she married again. Meanwhile, my parents sold their house and moved to Florida to retire. Linda's second marriage only lasted a few years as well and toward the end of it, she moved with her girls to Florida not far from my parents.

Chapter Forty-Four
2006

It's my first trip to Florida to see my sister since our parents died. Linda had a hard time finding a place to live after her recent break up with a boyfriend, and I want to see where she landed. We talked on the phone during her search for a place she could afford, and I tried to help from a distance as much as I could. But, ultimately all I could do was to help her meet the first two month's rent deposit. Any money from the settlement with the airline has long since been depleted and she relies on disability assistance because of her injuries. Her back and leg pain requires constant pain medication. She walks with the help of a cane, and uses a scooter for shopping and longer outings.

Coming from the West Palm Beach airport, I try to follow her directions, but I can't seem to find the street she told me she lives on. I call her on my cell, and she talks me through the turns until I see a small street between streets that looks like an alleyway. It's lined with small houses that look more like shacks to me. My heart sinks a little when I see her little red car parked in front of one of them. The one-story box-like building has yellow peeling paint and a flat unevenly shingled roof. It doesn't look big enough to have more than one room inside. One reason she chose the place was because it is on one level, and she can manage getting in and out with groceries and laundry.

Linda is at her door when I pull up. She looks small to me, slightly hunched over and leaning heavily on her cane. Her hair is short and reddish blonde and has thinned quite a bit. I can tell she's taken extra care with her makeup for me today and she's dressed in a colorful purple and white print top with black slacks. I notice she's wearing the silver earrings and necklace I gave her for her last birthday. She's glad to see me and we hug at the entrance way to her place. She looks well, if a little tired around her eyes. I watch her watch my face drop as I come inside and I try to hide my shock.

Linda has managed to make the place homey. The tiny kitchen only has space for a very small table with two chairs. Linda proudly shows me how she has painted a kitchen set she found discarded in a dumpster. There is a living room of sorts, where I spot many familiar things from her old place as well as some things from my parents' home: an antique cigarette holder; the Royal Dalton pitcher I brought her back from England; a white vase that my mother made in ceramics. The couch is another pick-up that someone discarded, with a blanket thrown over it to dress it up. She has hung pictures on the wall and gotten some lamps to counteract the darkness of the place. The one window in the room is boarded up.

She's made a pot of coffee and bought a cake to celebrate my arrival and we sit at her kitchen table for a while and talk. This place is not permanent, she tells me. Just until she can find a better one. We talk about how to find one and I offer some ideas about newspaper listings and using the Web. I ask her if she wants to go out and look at some places while I'm here. She can see I am anxious to get her out of this place. All I can think of is how upset my parents would be to see her here.

We get around to talking about my writing, and I tell her what I've been doing, how I've been collecting articles, going through our parents' letters and hers to me. I take out a folder I brought with me and we uncover some of the details together. In various news articles, we find that the plane hit #306 and #310 Williamson nearly simultaneously. Number 306 exploded and collapsed, the sides of the house falling outward, the people inside buried.

As the flames roared through my parents building, it also spread through the duplex frame house next door and the concrete house behind them. A car exploded inside a garage.

Rosa Caruso was the lone survivor of #306 – pulled out of her flaming kitchen by Patrolmen John Mannion and John Long. Her husband was still inside.

The third floor of my parent's building was completely destroyed. Neither Michael nor Christina Pagoulatos got out. Their boarder, Karl Reuling Jr., missed the crash by those 10 minutes he kept his class after school.

All of the children got out of the candy store, on the ground floor of my parents' building, unharmed. The owners of the store, Alfred and Margaret Collins had a near-tragic confusion. Margaret was behind the soda fountain and thought Alfred was in the back. Their niece, who was waitressing, dragged Margaret out as she screamed, "He's in there! Alfred is in there!" But he wasn't. He was standing outside the building waiting for her.

Linda and I ruminate about the 'what ifs.'

"If that day hadn't been foggy and rainy, Donna wouldn't have been home. She would have stayed at school to do her project," Linda says.

"Well, there may never have been the crash in the first place then," I add.

"You know, Dad always thought it would have come out different if he had been home when it happened," she says.

"I can't see how."

I leave Linda's house and get back into my rental car and head for my hotel. I'm feeling so close to the accident, looking at it with Linda, and still seeing the ramifications of the crash in her life. Thinking about the place she is living now, I have to pull my car over to just let the tears have their way. Still, I have trouble accepting the unfairness, and the contrast in our lives. As I think about how grateful I am to be going home tomorrow to my raised ranch, my husband and my son, I'm hit with a familiar wave of guilt.

Chapter Forty-Five
JANUARY 22, 1952
DAY OF THE CRASH
3:40 PM

Captain Reid's plane was cleared to 2,500 feet, then 1,500 feet. He was told to start his approach and was cleared for landing at 3:45 pm on Newark Runway 6.

My mother checked the kitchen clock to time her baking, watched the second hand bounce and tick the minutes away. Her bright yellow curtains let in as much light as the gray day offered. The black and white tiled floor caught a glint by her feet. Her shoes clicked on the tile as she moved from sink to stove to refrigerator.

Donna and Sheila had spread poster boards for their science project on jet propulsion on the floor and were outlining letters in marker. They were quietly engrossed in their work, their markers squeaking across the shiny surface.

Linda was supposed to be napping on the couch in the living room, but instead was playing with measuring cups, contentedly fitting them together and taking them apart to hear the clang of metal on metal.

"What smells so good Mrs. M?" Sheila asked.

"Come on girls, come sit and have some chocolate chip cookies. They're still warm. Tell me how your day was."

Donna and Sheila took seats at the kitchen table. My mother poured two glasses of milk.

Chapter Forty-Six
PESTY

"That finger won't be worth a damn. It won't ever bend. And, it may cause infection. She would do just fine without it. It will just be a pest for her," the doctor said.

Amputation was his recommendation for three-year-old Linda's left index finger. The joint of the finger was fused, contracted by a patchwork of thick, discolored scar tissue. A stick of a finger with a tiny rock of nail tipping the edge.

"With everything she is going through, I don't want to take anything more away from her," was my mother's reasoning when she told the doctor no.

And so, "pesty" was named and adopted as a favored digit. A pet that was babied and cared for. The small nail chip polished in bright red with each manicure. Pesty was a symbol of defiance and gut decisions that were often necessary.

"Sometimes, we just know best," my mother would say.

Chapter Forty-Seven **2006**

I'm at Linda's new apartment in Florida, a vast improvement over the last one. This one is small but cozy, in a two family house with a small yard for her little toy poodle to run outside. It's clean and everything in it works. It has a real roof and real windows that let light inside, though I worry about the ventilation and how much Linda smokes. She is limping badly now. Although she tries to hide it, I see her wince when she stands from her chair.

It's no mystery now that her knee replacement a few years ago was too big for her leg. By the time it was discovered to be the problem, no surgeon wanted to do the re-replacement because of complications with her scar tissue. I don't want her to give up on finding a solution to her pain and urged her to see another doctor. I asked my doctor in Connecticut to recommend a surgeon down here and she has just seen him. This new doctor has told Linda that he will do it, but that there is a 50% chance he will have to amputate her leg if he encounters problems with the surgery. And he anticipates problems.

We're sitting on her couch talking it over, her dog running between us for attention. I am a poor substitute for my mother. She would have known the right thing to say, how to advise her. I flounder with the words.

"They're doing wonderful things with prostheses these days," I tell her. The words escape before I catch their meaning. They fall with a thud between us.

"Let's do some online research," I offer. "See what some of the support groups say." About amputees, I don't say.

The knee doesn't bend anymore. A stick of a leg. A painful pest of a leg. But, she decides it's better to have it than risk losing it.

I look down and see that the nails on the foot of the offending leg are painted with bright red polish.

Chapter Forty-Eight
JANUARY 22, 1952
Day of the Crash
3:41 PM

Flight 6780 was over Linden, below 1500-feet, and was again advised to listen to Newark radar. Captain Reid seemed to be drifting on and off his flight plan course.

This was the recorded interchange at 3:41 pm:

"American 6780, this is Newark radar. How do you hear? Over."

"Roger, radar, I've been listening to you monitor 6720 and I hear you loud and clear." 6720 was another American Airlines Convair immediately ahead of 6780. It landed safely on Runway 6 at Newark at 3:39 pm.

"6780, this is Newark radar, I have you 5 ½ miles out, coming up on the glide path and you're 900 feet to the left of course."

"American 6780, 5 miles out, on the glide path, still 900 feet to the left of course."

"Coming back to course now, you're now 400 feet left, glide path is good 4 ½ miles out."

At four miles out, radar control sent the message:

"300 feet to the left and coming back to course."

"Right on course, and 100 feet high on the glide path with the courthouse one mile ahead."

The Elizabeth courthouse was three quarters of a mile from my parents' home on Williamson Street.

Then, from radar control:

"...you're drifting to the right, you're 900 feet to the right of course and ½ mile from the Court House."

Four or five seconds later, the aircraft vanished from radar screens.

Several requests were sent to Flight 6780 for its position. None were answered.

Chapter Forty-Nine
1954

Linda started kindergarten at the same school that Donna had attended, Woodrow Wilson School 19. My mother walked her there, along the same streets, but from a different direction now. I was just four months old.

On the way to her class, Linda passed this memorial plaque on the wall near the principal's office:

In loving memory of our friend and classmate
Donna Jo Mandel
July 25, 1945 – January 22, 1952

At first, she felt like a sort of star at school. Everyone knew her, and of the accident, and her sister – now famous in her death. She didn't have the chance not to tell anyone. She wore the evidence every day.

Photos of Linda at that age showed a spunky kid with a ready smile and a determined look in her eye. My parents had put everything into building her confidence, showing her all the things she could accomplish just by trying hard. Already, she had learned to walk twice; once at a year old, and again at three after the accident. In a few years, she would have to do it again after another surgery.

My mother started working with the PTA the year before Linda started school, while she was pregnant with me, arranging seminars and workshops with parents and teachers about what today would be called "diversity." She kept encouraging class discussions about accepting people that were different in some way. She used the PTA as a tool to make Linda's life easier.

Her early school years were good ones. In first grade, Linda even got her first real valentine. But, later, kids were not as accepting, and were sometimes cruel. When teenagers started having parties where the boys and girls would pair off, Linda told me, she was left alone. She would go to the bathroom a lot, or help in the kitchen to get out of the situation and then go home to cry herself to sleep. Finally, she wouldn't go to those parties at all, making up some excuse to my parents– that her friends wouldn't be there, or she had something else to do.

I must have realized some of this happened while it occurred, but Linda made so light of it, that it was easy to ignore. She was always fine, she said, whenever I asked.

Chapter Fifty
2006

With Justin away at college, this is the first time David and I have lived alone together in our six years of marriage. Although I miss my son in an almost physical way, this part of the empty nest equation is a nice one. David and I can be just a couple, which we have never really had a chance to be. We can just be us. It's the kind of calm, happy relationship I always hoped to find.

I'm thinking of how my parents survived what they did. I decide to do some research into grief and, specifically, the death of a child. Online I find a plethora of books to order that promise some answers on the subject along with some online support groups. I wish these had been around for my parents, my mother especially, to help them through.

While I'm reading about how parents try to recover from losing a child, I find that many decide to have another child, and then I see a term I had never seen: replacement child. Though the words are used to describe an antidote for the parents, the children themselves seem to be at some risk in their role as healers. They even have a psychiatric condition named for them: Replacement Child Syndrome.

Chapter Fifty-One
JANUARY 22, 1952
DAY OF THE CRASH

3:43 PM

A few blocks away from my parents' house, Vincent J. O'Connell was standing in his yard at 325 Fay Avenue. He heard the aircraft approach from the southeast. Several seconds later, he heard a loud blast or backfire, and then another after a few more seconds.

By that time, the aircraft was close to where he stood and veered sharply to the right. It was over his head when there was a third blast. He saw a yellowish glare for a moment through the fog.

"One motor stopped. The other increased in intensity and whined," he told reporters. It seemed, "as if a tremendous amount of power was being applied." A few seconds later – "a terrific explosion in the distance."

The plane careened just over the rooftop of Battin High and landed across the street. Cafeteria workers were sure the blast was an atomic bomb. The 300 students inside escaped the crash by 50 yards.

In the tiny concrete house behind my parents, Mrs. Fetske heard a roar, and then one wall of the building fell away. She grabbed her baby, Albert, and escaped.

At #314, Mrs. William Schwartz raced with the baby she was watching, and her own two children across the street to the high school.

Selma Kurtzer, Beverly Chessler and Leona Lewis arrived home safely just as the plane hit, thanks to my mother sending them home from their rehearsal when she did.

Having dismissed the possibility of a second crash in their vicinity only a half-hour earlier, nurses at St. Elizabeth's Hospital heard Flight 6780 zoom overhead, then crash a block from their maternity and children's wards.

John Delaney, Chaplain at St. Elizabeth's also ran to the scene. As he got close, he heard screams from inside the plane. They quieted quickly.

Captain Reid's wife looked out her window to see a plane flying low, lower, disappearing into the row of houses the next street over. She heard the moment of impact, saw the explosions.

Chapter Fifty-Two **1972**

When I went away to college at The University of Hartford in Connecticut, I can't say that I was any different from any other 18 year old in wanting to be off on my own, but I felt a certain urgency to get away. It was almost like I needed to be away from my family to survive as an individual, and to escape some underlying expectation that I could not identify. The school was far enough away from home, three hours by car, to avoid the 'drop-in' visit from my parents, and close enough to drive home for holidays and the occasional weekend.

Music was taking a back seat by the time I went to college. I majored in theatre, even though I had never landed a part in any play in high school. Nevertheless, ever since seeing Patty Duke in *The Miracle Worker*, I had decided that I could become anyone I wanted to be through acting. My first semester I jumped at the chance to go to England with my theatre class. We saw an average of two plays a day for two weeks in London. On the weekends we took tours of historic sites and travelled in the countryside. The trip opened my eyes to the larger world and made me want to broaden my experiences.

In the spring semester of my freshman year at college I met transfer student from England in my fencing class. Steven was the opposite of any boy I'd ever met. He was tall, blonde and bearded.

When he called and asked me if I liked the theatre, I reminded him that I was a theatre major – so, of course I liked the theatre. He had tickets for The Hartford Stage Company for Saturday–would I like to go?

I was impressed that this would be a real date, not a walk back to my dorm after a mixer dance. That night I put on a pair of slacks–not jeans – excited to be going to the city in Hartford to see a play.

The play was Noel Coward's Private Lives. The whole farce is about a combative, if humorous, marriage with interchanges like this one:

> "What is so horrible that one can't stay happy . . ."
>
> "How long will it last, this ludicrous, overbearing love of ours?"
>
> "Who knows."
>
> "Shall we always want to bicker and fight?"
>
> "No, that desire will fade, along with our passion."

Steven was preoccupied with showing me how much he knew about Noel Coward while I was trying to follow the fast-moving dialogue and I missed half of the double entendres trying to listen to him at the same time. By the end of the play I was mostly annoyed.

On the way home, Steven looked down at the gas gauge and announced, "I guess I should have stopped for gas this afternoon. Looks like we're out."

He pulled over to the curb in an unsavory part of the city. At least 10 hooded teenagers blocked the entrance to a convenience store, passing a bottle and laughing. They nudged each other when the bottle stopped for too long. The sidewalk was littered with empty cans, bottles and burger wrappers.

Steven said. "Wait here. I'll go call my father to help us out."

The convenience store guys watched him get out of the car and spotted me in the passenger seat. I was scared to be left alone in the car. Steven gave them a "hi" sign, making his way to the pay phone. I was cursing under my breath when he finally got back to the car, really upset that he had left me alone with these thugs leering at me.

"He'll be here in a minute. Sorry about this."

When we said goodnight, I jumped from the car before the awkward moment of a possible kiss goodnight, said "thanks for the evening" and "see you in class tomorrow," and walked resolutely to my dorm without looking back. Although I saw him in fencing class, we didn't date again that semester.

But that summer he called me out of the blue. He would be driving through New Jersey the following weekend, he said, and wanted to stop by. I agreed to see him – I was having a boring summer, working at a law office as a gopher.

His visit was very different from our date. He picked me up from work one day and drove me home. Then, we went out to a local diner for something to eat and we talked for hours about everything – about how we wanted to travel and try new ways of living our lives. We seemed to want the same things out of life. My family warmed to him, which also changed how I saw him. The contrast of seeing him in my home with my family just exaggerated his exoticness.

He was headed for Africa the next week on a photographic safari.

"I only shoot animals with my camera," he liked to say.

It was his letters from Africa that captivated me and gave me the rush of freedom I was looking for. He described hot-red sunsets over the endless expanse of dense jungle, waterbuck that wandered into his camp, the thrill of getting a close-up of a rhino. Through his letters, I felt like I was there, cooking with him on the camp stove in the black night, startling at the howls of distant hyenas. By September, I was sorry I would not be returning to college with him in Connecticut. I had transferred to the University of West Virginia for their theatre program and to explore a new part of the country.

"I'll visit," he promised.

I didn't count on it, knowing it was a 14-hour drive from Hartford.

That semester, though, Steven wore out his '65 Mustang driving to see me every weekend. And I failed my Friday 8 a.m. Forestry class since he always arrived on Thursday nights.

In October, we camped out with some friends in the Blue Ridge Mountains. Walking through the cathedral-like ceiling of golden leaves in the lavish woods was spiritual; a new religion of fresh green calm in the ethereal light of sunrise. The natural beauty seemed to frame the whole weekend in a transcendent glow.

Late that Saturday afternoon, I stumbled headlong into the lake. When Steven caught me in his arms and gently carried me up the embankment, I truly fell. We didn't have sex that night, but sleeping warmly cuddled together in his sleeping bag was almost more intimate for me.

After that we talked about taking our relationship to the next level, the physical one, and the next weekend, I cajoled a friend into lending us her apartment. The bed, with a thick quilt of reds, blues and greens, took up the entire bedroom. We had to crawl over it to get into or out of the room.

Cat Stevens played on the small stereo.

"Oooh baby, baby, it's a wild world. . ."

We sipped wine and breathed each other's essence, his the scent of vanilla as I rested my head on his chest. We reveled in each other, finding new ways our bodies fit together under the multi-colored quilt. Experimenting to the point of exhaustion. Sleeping, waking and making love again and again. I don't recall taking any other nourishment that weekend.

The next July, Steven got a summer job that promised to provide the journey across America that he had always wanted. He would be travelling the country buying scrap metal from dentists, who saved all the gold and silver dug from their patients' teeth. I couldn't imagine being away from him all summer, and so I hopped a bus to Philadelphia one night to meet him, leaving my poor parents a note. When I called them from Philadelphia, my mother sounded resigned and my father recited his usual "be careful" and asked me to call every few days.

On that trip, I saw parts of the country I may never have seen. It felt at times like we were transported back 100 years when we stopped in one-horse towns in the mid-west that had only a diner, a gas station and a general store. I found it hard to believe these places still existed in 1973. We navigated miles and miles of corn, every road flat and endless.

We crossed each state border like Marco Polo – looking for the intrigue, noting the characters at the diner counter, the texture of life there. Steven somehow knew the right roads and the right stops to make and I began to think of him as my life guide. I attributed his cool reserve to his being English, a cultural trait, and figured that I could change that tendency in time. Again, I found myself defining myself from his vision of me. I was an explorer. I was courageous. I was Steven's girl.

When our red Chevy was laden with gold and silver, the car tilted at a 45-degree angle and shocks threatening to break, we headed back east. I ditched my plans to return to West Virginia and attended a local college instead so that I could live at home while Steven finished up his degree in Connecticut. My parents seemed oddly quiet and accepting about my decision.

Chapter Fifty-Three
2006

I'm staring out at the maple tree over the top of my computer screen in my home office. It snowed this morning and the branches are dipped in white. There's a huge black crow sitting alone on a branch at eye level, staring me down. He's probably cawing, but I can't hear him through my closed, frosted window. My cat has just spotted the bird too, and is stalking him on the windowsill.

I'm scanning through the pile of books I ordered online about grief and recovery from the loss of a child. And, about replacement children.

I first turn to Freud to try to get a sense of how my parents may have dealt with the grief of losing Donna. He said that grieving *involves grave departures from the normal attitude to life, and yet it never occurs to us to regard it as a pathological condition and to refer it to medical treatment. Instead, we look to its being overcome after a certain lapse of time.*[1]

I read further that it's probable that Donna's sudden and traumatic death, the destruction of all her possessions, and her very bedroom were all factors that robbed my parents of some of the usual forms of grieving.

For my mother, the ache of losing Donna never went away. In a way, I don't think she wanted it to. Her grief was her secret child. She nurtured it, fed it with melancholy, clothed it in her depression.

I could not adequately understand my mother's grief until I had my own child, and felt first hand how the child that was once part of your body remains an essential part of your being.

I know she tried over the years to rise above the hurt of losing Donna. In the mornings she would say to us, "I can't go out yet, I have to put on my "face."

Her "face" consisted of delicately applying highlights under her eyes, a demur line of brown outlining them, the pale cream foundation for an even palette. But, for her, it was more than a figure of speech or her makeup – it was her mask. Often, it worked and she believed what she saw in the mirror. Other times, the happy mask stood out grotesquely against her inner reality. A sad clown with a painted smile.

My father, I believe, did his grieving in private. He also medicated himself with comic relief, which ultimately gave some balance to my parents' relationship. Victor Borges said, "Laughter is the shortest distance between two people." And so it was for my mother and father. With an innate understanding of this truth, my father kept my mother from disappearing into the kind of tragedy that could have swallowed any joy.

The research book I ordered about Replacement Child Syndrome just came in the mail and I rip open the padded envelope. I read that replacement children often feel they can never live up to the memory of the dead child.

I recognize myself in some of the descriptions of those with this affliction: guilt; a wavering sense of identity; the feeling of responsibility to measure up. In my case, it was guilt at being spared from the crash – from death, but also from Linda's injury. There was a feeling of responsibility throughout my childhood that I needed to be the one who was easy to care for, that no one had to worry about. This, even as I may have resented the extra attention Linda needed.

After reading about how complicated the syndrome can be for children, I think my parents did well at letting me be an individual in my own right. Some parents never fully separate the replacement from the replaced in their own minds and even continue to dress the child in the dead child's clothes, name them with the same name, and fully expect them to become that lost child. After some ill-fated hairstyles early on, my mother let go of that expectation for me. My father, too, did the best he could at letting me be me, though I feel he wanted Donna to be here in my place. In any case, I never felt, as some replacements do, that I needed to become Donna.

Chapter Fifty-Four
JANUARY 22, 1952
The Crash

3:45 pm

A low roar. Sputtering cracks of backfire. Explosion. Screams.

Witnesses all remembered the sounds. My mother didn't.

She saw the flash of fire, her children in flames.

My mother's world came crashing down, literally through her roof. The fire burst from nothing. In an instant, the kitchen was a collage of white-red, blue-yellow against black smoke. Her canary yellow walls faded into gray, crumbled to black. A metallic fume filled her nostrils, her eyes stung and teared. The blast had thrown my mother flat on the linoleum, the floor rumbling beneath her. She felt the heat on top of her, insistently pressing her to stay down. She glanced up to see one clear passage way to safety – down the front stairs to the street.

Fleetingly, she thought "The oil burner has exploded!" But, that was located at the front of the building. It made no sense. She heard screams, and realized that some were her own. Her mind ceased making rational meaning of the scene and her instinct took over. Her own mother was sprawled just feet in front of her.

"Run!" my mother screamed at her. "Run Mom, don't ask questions!" She grabbed her mother's arm and hurried her down the front stairs. Hermina, my grandmother, bewildered, stumbled out the door to safety.

Turning back, my mother saw that her daughter's visiting friend, Sheila, was on fire, she threw a rug around her to smother the flames and pushed her toward the door. Sheila ran outside to safety, though badly burned.

The fire rushed through the apartment, rolling in on a carpet of thick, white smoke toward the stairway. The screams and cries of her children rose above the crackling roar of the fast moving fire.

Chapter Fifty-Five
1974

It was Valentine's Day when Steven asked me to marry him. I was 20 and still living at home, going to school nearby, and he came down from Connecticut for the weekend. When he brought me home from dinner that evening, we sat my parents down in the kitchen and told them the news. Steven had brought a bottle of wine for the occasion. He popped the cork and I fetched some wine glasses from my mother's dining room hutch. After our toast, I sensed something was amiss in our happy announcement and glanced over at my father studying his wine glass. My mother was looking his way as well. He looked upset about something, although I was oblivious to what it was. My mother motioned for me to come into the hallway with her.

"Your father expected Steven to ask him first," she explained. "Before he proposed, he should've asked for your hand."

I was a little annoyed. This was 1974 after all. It was *my* hand.

But after seeing the disappointment in my father's eyes, I went to Steven.

"You need to ask him," I said. "It's ridiculous, but he's hurt. You have to do it."

In the interest of equality and feminism, I went with him. The three of us settled downstairs in the family room. The room had a theater theme. Gold masks of comedy and tragedy hung over the couch on either side of a print of a grand costume ball, with a jester at its center. The lamp on the side table looked just like the jester in the picture.

Steven was positioned on the brown tweed couch against the long wall with my father and I on the matching love seat perpendicular to him. My father took a sip of his coffee and put his cup on the round mica table in front of him. He sat back with his arms folded.

The jester lamp was poking up behind Steven's head as he spoke in quiet tones that underscored his English accent. I wrestled a nervous giggle to the pit of my stomach.

"Mr. Mandel, I'm so sorry we didn't come to you first..."

The jester grinned, his eyes masked in black, the toreador hat perched at an angle.

Then my father and my fiancée stood facing each other, shaking hands.

"Take good care of my little girl," my father looked him in the eye, a steady laser gaze.

"Of course I will, Mr. Mandel. You can count on that."

The deal made, my father put his arm around Steven's shoulder in conspiracy, turned him away from me.

"And, don't worry son, she'll fill out in a few years, you'll see. Her mother was as skinny as a rail when I married her. Now look at her," he said, cupping his hands in front of his chest in the universal sign for large breasts.

We were a very idealistic young married couple. After the wedding and a short road trip of a honeymoon, we went back to Connecticut to find jobs and an apartment. I had quit college to get married, so job opportunities were not plentiful for me. I got a clerical job in Hartford at a brokerage firm and Steven started working for an ad agency that sold space on the side of VW bugs. Neither of us was living out our dreams. Steven had set his sites on broadcasting, and I wanted to break into music to sing.

One day, we both came home from work and sat silently at our tiny kitchen table, unable to find a way to explain our day to each other, when I blurted out, "I got fired." Steven one-upped me, "I punched my boss in the face." He had a better excuse than I did. I was just a lousy clerical worker. Steven had hit his boss when he said he had married me just to get a green card to stay in the States. We agreed then that we would support each other if either of us found a way to go after what we wanted.

After that I found work in a music store and met some musicians who encouraged me to start singing and playing guitar at coffee shops and clubs in the area. Steven would come with me, setting up my equipment and watching out for me. He was very supportive at the start, but it got difficult for him when he got a day job in a department store. Eventually, there were nights he couldn't make it, or would leave early to get some sleep.

In a year or so I quit the music store job and joined a full time band. Again, Steven was behind the decision. I had put down the guitar and was concentrating on being a lead singer. The first band I was in played locally, so I was home most nights. Later, though, I joined a cover band that travelled up and down the east coast playing the hotel circuit. I was away for weeks at a time. By then, Steven was working at an insurance company full time. I knew he was frustrated with the job, and the mundane path he seemed to be on. He began to pull away from me, both emotionally and physically, and I was starting to think that I could never make him happy. I was losing the feeling that filled the hole in my self-esteem. When my young husband pulled away, it was like my father's indifference all over again. I think it was then that I started subconsciously looking for someone new to give me the validation I needed.

Chapter Fifty-Six 2006 Letters From My Father

It is extremely cold today in New England. The cold brings a profound quiet to the neighborhood. No children are playing basketball in the driveways, or street hockey outside my window after school.

I'm reading through letters from my father. He had such beautiful handwriting, and – surprisingly – was the better of my parents at expressing his emotions on paper. Whenever I find one of his letters to me, buried in a sock drawer or folded in among my jewelry, I wind up blubbering at his words. I never heard these kinds of thoughts from his own lips, and never knew them as a child. Almost all of his letters to me were written after I was an adult, and most after he was 70. Each of them ends with the warning to "be careful" about something I'm about to do, or am involved in at the time.

As I look back now, many of his letters still defined me in terms of my sister:

> *Even when we felt you were being neglected you showed strength and understanding to love Linda as much as we did, and to show that love to her.*

Or, I was their hope, their healer, that he finally learned to love:

> *One of the greatest gifts given to us at an essential time of our lives was when the gods delivered you into our hearts and lives. Your birth helped sustain us with some faith and hope. It's taken me a lifetime – but you've taught me to say it and feel it – I love you and it's forever.*

I was a compromise, a gamble, a winning bet:

> *I compromised. I told mother we'd try one time–and if it takes–ok. If not, we'll just continue with God's plan. So, you see, you really are one of God's special children.*

That was the dichotomy that characterized my relationship with my father. Surely he thought about the fact that I would not be here if Donna had lived. So, any love for me was a kind of betrayal. I was alternately a blessing and a painful reminder of her. Although I looked like her, I was flawed by a lazy eye. I was good, but could never be *as* good, *as* kind, *as* exceptional as Donna. How could I be?

Sometimes I fantasized that I was Donna reincarnated. The true replacement child, in disguise.

Judy in disguise – with glasses.

Chapter Fifty-Seven
JANUARY 22, 1952
The Crash

3:45 pm

Linda had been playing in the living room in the back of the apartment when the plane hit and she was instantly engulfed in flame. Donna was in the kitchen in the front of the apartment. My mother was between the rooms by the stairway after getting her mother and Sheila out the door.

"Get the baby!" Donna screamed. "The baby is on fire!"

My mother tried to see where her voice was coming from, but the smoke was so thick she couldn't see Donna in the kitchen. She could not see her face. Later, she was grateful for this small blessing, that she would not be haunted by the image of her daughter's last expression, the fear in her eyes, before she had to abandon her.

"Donna, run!" my mother ordered over to Donna as she ran to the living room. "Down to the front door, it's the only way out!"

My mother saw no movement from Donna and was momentarily angry at her daughter's defiance. Then she saw that Donna's leg was wedged under the fallen beam that caught her before she could run. One of the crumbled brick walls of the structure rested on top of the beam. She weighed some 51 lbs. The beam and debris trapping her was easily 100 times her weight.

For a moment that passed like hours, my mother was frozen, torn between her two children. To run to the baby, or to help free Donna. Neither choice could be the right one. But, making none would condemn them both. She knew she had to move.

Finally, she let Donna choose and followed her older daughter's plea to go to two-year-old Linda.

Reaching the living room, her heart seemed to stop when she saw the ball of flame that was her baby. Linda had stopped screaming. The quilt lying on the sofa was untouched, and she wrapped Linda in it and rolled her on the floor to put out the flames, ignoring the burns that now scorched her own hands. Then, she rolled the baby down the stairs that led to the outside front door. She turned back to get Donna, but before she could take a step she heard the click of the door lock at the bottom of the stairs. With the door locked, she knew that no one would be able to open the door to retrieve Linda now lying just inside the door. She rushed down to the door – a move she questioned for the rest of her life – and released Linda into the arms of a man there. The stranger there was Henry Shubecz, who happened to be driving by when the plane crashed directly in front of him. He took Linda's motionless body from my mother, smoke rising from inside the blanket, and saw the black charred skin and red burnt flesh, peeking out. The smell slapped at him like a hand against his chest.

My mother turned to go back inside when she felt a strong arm on hers. Seeing the ferocious flames consuming the stairway, Henry held her back, saving her life. Two passing patrolmen soon joined him to help restrain my mother just as the wooden staircase snapped, crackled like kindling and collapsed with the second floor. Henry handed the baby off to Reverend Shoenborn, suddenly there by his side, who carefully cradled Linda.

Donna heard my mother go to Linda and run down the stairs. She waited for her to come back to help her. She was having trouble breathing through the suffocating cover of smoke and strained to see my mother's figure emerge from the hot clouds.

In her seven short years, Donna always relied on the steady protection of my parents. My mother was always there to curl her hair, kiss the cuts on her knees, console her disappointments. She had no reason to doubt the outcome of any dire situation, even this last one. She trusted – even as the flames closed in around her. She felt the heat on her torso and arms as she pulled at her mutinous leg, willing it to move. She heard a whoosh of fire, the crackling of burning wood, faint screams in the distance and smelled her own burning flesh mixed with the fumes of jet fuel. As the flames began to envelope her face, and she lost consciousness in the smoke filled apartment, Donna still believed my mother would rescue her.

Outside, my mother's screams merged with Donna's –
"Mommy, help me Mommy, Mommy. . ." – until they stopped.
My mother collapsed in a heap on the hot pavement.

Making his way through the gathering crowd on Williamson Street, Reverend Schoenborn carried Linda across to the Battin High gym. At that point, it was only a holding area for the injured, a morgue for the dead.

Ambulances had not yet arrived. All the Reverend could do was to hold Linda to keep her warm–and pray.

My mother, in shock, was being led from the burning building by her defacto caregivers who had no hope of controlling her screams.

Ambulances raced from four surrounding towns to rush victims to St. Elizabeth's Hospital.

My father was replacing a tray of watches in the front window of his store when he heard sirens and people yelling on the street.

"It's another plane crash!"

A phone call from a neighbor confirmed his fear, "You better get home Al!"

He forgot his car was parked across the street and ran home.

When he got to his neighborhood, it was a war zone of chaos. Ambulances were loading the injured and burned. Three fire engines lined the street as firemen fought the flames that shot out from the windows of his building and filled the air with black clouds. He couldn't see into the opaque blocks of smoke that filled the windows.

He spotted my mother on a stretcher, being lifted into an ambulance. When he called out, she did not respond.

After he identified himself as her husband, the paramedic told him that their baby daughter had been rushed to St. Elizabeth's Hospital. The ambulance door slammed shut, sirens screamed. My father watched it pull away without a word. Nearby, he heard a reporter say to someone, "…little girl in critical condition."

Staring up at the scorched remnants of his home, surrounded by melee, my father began to grasp the reality. And where was Donna? Was she still at school? Did she run? His mind raced.

He found a fireman and grabbed his arm.

"I have two daughters, one was taken to the hospital. I can't find the other. She's seven."

"One child was trapped on the second floor, didn't make it out. Is that your apartment?" The fireman pointed to the second floor.

My father could not breathe. The fireman caught him just as his knees gave way and lowered him to the curb.

When he mustered his will to look up again, my father saw no evidence of a plane. It looked more like a bomb had hit the row of houses.

He asked the fireman, "Did you see a little girl running away?"

"Everyone who escaped is at Battin High."

Pouncing on this hope, my father headed across the street.

The school gym, being used for triage, had the look of a battleground. The injured were strewn around the room as paramedics moved quickly from one to another, their quiet work punctuated by moans. Bloodied bandages were piled in heaps. Gurneys were loaded and wheeled across the hardwood floor, sounding like muffled machine gun fire. My father walked slowly around the gymnasium, searching each young face for Donna. The back of one little girl's head looked like her, but as she turned her face to him, his hope was dashed.

The neighbors, he thought, Donna ran to a neighbor's house. Maybe the Earlman's up the street. He found a phone in the school office and dialed all the neighbors within walking distance but got no answers.

Back out on the street, he scrutinized each window of his home for signs of life.

"Al Mandel?" He heard a voice and a fireman touched his arm.

"Al, you should be at the hospital. We'll look for your daughter, and someone will find you."

My father walked toward the hospital.

Chapter Fifty-Eight
1975 - 1979

I was travelling with my most recent band on my 21st birthday. The band was staying in an old farmhouse in Troy, NY. It was a white clapboard with a wrap-around porch and a big backyard. A small kitchen saved us considerable money on food. I had one of the four bedrooms to myself, and I commandeered one of the bathrooms. We drove 40 minutes every night to our gig at the Top Hat bar. We usually played at Hiltons and Marriotts, but this job was a low point in our tour. The bar was a run-down establishment where we actually performed on the top of a bar that had been converted to a makeshift stage. Dancing in four-inch heals on the slippery surface was a risky balancing act each night.

The guys in the band were pretty good about having a "chick" with them. They treated me like their sister for the most part. Except our lead guitarist. I had to keep an eye on him.

Early on the morning of my birthday I took off for a drive by myself, looking for some way to make the day special. Even living this kind of non-structured life, I was beginning to feel too complacent, like it was all getting to be too 'normal.' On this birthday especially I wanted to strike out and feel some adrenaline, and know that I wasn't playing it safe even if that was what my parents had tried to instill in me. They were still reeling from the fact that I was travelling alone with five men.

I spotted an airfield in the distance and aimed for it. A sign out in front read GLIDER RIDES $25.00! A steep price since I was only making $200 a week, but the idea of the flight called to me. Flying on a whisp of wind would be just the thing to set the tone for my 21st year.

There were six small planes lining the runway. I found a small man inside a small building on the strip.

"How do the glider rides work?" I asked.

"Hi, I'm Ed," he said, extending his hand. "Come on over and take a look."

Ed walked me over to a sleek white plane that sat low to the ground. The wingspan seemed three times wider than the other planes. Very narrow, very long. The cockpit had just enough room for one person. Behind it was a second cockpit with it's own controls. He pointed to that one.

"You sit back there and I sit up front. Another plane with an engine," he laughed, "tows us up to 3,000 feet, finds a good gust of wind and lets us go."

The glider had no propellers of its own.

"What happens if the wind stops?" I asked Ed.

"We just find the right current and drift back down to the airstrip. Or we drop like a rock!" Ed was quite the comedian.

It was starting to warm up from the cool morning. A few white puffs dotted the deep blue sky.

"Ok. When can I go up?" I handed him my $25.

"Now is good."

Ed disappeared for ten minutes and returned with the pilot for the powered plane who taxied a Cessna up to the glider and maneuvered it in to attach a tether line.

He told me to hop in, but there was no door, so I lifted myself over the shallow side of the back cockpit and climbed over the stick in the middle.

"That stick is what makes us go up and down–in case you have to use it."

I was too paralyzed with fear to ask him why I would have to use it. The fear felt good. The risk made me feel alive.

I strapped myself in, put on a helmet and tested out the radio that let us talk to each other.

"Well, Judy, here we go," he said. "When we get up to altitude, I'm going to let you fly her for a while. How does that sound?"

"Great, really great," I said, my heart pounding in my throat.

Ed gave a thumbs-up to the Cessna. I listened to the engines wind up from a gradual *purr* to a full throttle crescendo. We were towed down the runway and were airborne in seconds.

The glider lifted lightly over the trees like a kite on a string.

"Ok, let 'er go!" Ed called to the Cessna pilot.

The engine noise faded and the Cessna dove down and away from us. I heard only a faint whoosh, a quiet wind as we rose higher off the horizon. The peaceful quiet took over my thoughts. More and more land came into my picture frame view as we soared upward, the expanse spreading out below me. I could see where each road led, where the ends were dead, where they circled back into themselves. It was a clear vision we never see from the ground, and gave me a swelling sense of control.

Ed dipped the left wing and we descended slowly, then rode a draft of wind to climb higher.

"I'm a little tired," Ed said when we were high above the clouds. "I'm going to let you have it now. Take hold of the steering wheel in front of you and just hold it straight to glide for a while. If you feel us going down too much, pull the stick toward you."

I turned the plane slowly to the right. The plane dipped down and I pulled up on the stick to rise in a rush of power.

I felt bright blue. Sun hot. Straining toward the top of the next current.

I tried to pinpoint exactly when it started. Was it when I began travelling with the band, or staying out late singing at local clubs? Was it when Steven got a job at an insurance company, and we inhabited different worlds; me sleeping until 2 pm and getting home at 4 am; him rising at 6 am to go to work at a desk?

When I thought of us in that small apartment in college, not being able to untangle from each others bodies long enough to go out for pizza, I was at a loss to understand what happened to us. I was blind to the warning signs after the first-lust of our new love started to ebb. I needed affection and reinforcement from him. A touch, a look, a word. Steven was removed; a cool island.

I knew something was wrong when we took a three-hour car trip and didn't say a word to each other. Usually, I would try to initiate some kind of conversation, but I decided to test out just how long he could go without speaking to me on this trip. My anger had begun to gestate into a fully formed monster when I started to count the weeks, then months, between having sex. The retreat fed every seed of insecurity that my father had planted. I wasn't attractive enough, not smart enough, not worthy of love.

As we lost some vital connection, we would not speak for days at a time. When I reached for him, he would pull away. He would feign sleep when I came to bed. He would turn his head when I approached. He was unhappy, and I couldn't fix it. Then, he hatched a plan to go to South America to be a photographer for National Geographic – without me. That plan never materialized, but the thought of it had driven a wedge between us. I was hurt that he'd even considered it. When he decided to take some time, alone, to think things through, our marriage began an unstoppable unraveling.

I was singing at a lounge in a hotel nearby our Connecticut home at the time, just after Steven had moved out. When a guy at the bar started talking me up, I was ripe for an adventure. Gary was a pilot and told me how only a short drive away there was a place to skydive. I had another vodka and tonic.

"It's fantastic!" Gary, told me. "We take up around 15 skydivers and they all jump out together for a freefall. Then we dive the plane fast to get out of their way, or we might wing a few. You'll love it!"

I wasn't sure if I should take the trip with this man I barely knew, but when he described it, I felt a chill down the back of my neck, and I knew I would say yes.

Before I knew it, I was in some kind of military cargo plane. It had a giant hatchback that opened from the top with a ramp for driving in trucks, tanks and large equipment.

The jumpers piled into the back of the plane, laughing and talking loudly. Their bright orange, red and yellow jumpsuits rustled against the gray walls.

Gary strapped me in and helped me put on a helmet.

We climbed quickly to 10,000 feet, high enough for the free-fall, in the cloudless summer sky. I had a mile-wide view in the co-pilot seat: a thrush of green; black strips of road; brown and white brush stroke buildings. Straight ahead, a deep blue pallet. For a while, I recognized some landmarks – the highway, the airport, the center of the town. Then it all blurred to small dots and lines.

"Ready guys?" Gary said through the loudspeaker to the back of the plane. "I'll give you a count of ten. Try to jump one right after the other so you don't get separated. You have plenty of space up here."

He counted them down and I felt the weight of the plane shift as they jumped one by one. We lurched into a straight down dive.

"Hold on, Jude."

I felt like my ears were going to explode and I pulled on Gary's sleeve for help.

"Hold your nose and blow–it will relieve the pressure. Like this."

I did – and it worked.

We circled the jumpers from a safe quarter mile distance. I could see them holding hands in their circular formation. A marionette sky sculpture, floating in slow motion, suspended from nothing. Then, all at once, they let go their hands, separated, and pulled their chutes, looking like slices of rainbow cutting the bright blue.

Chapter Fifty-Nine
2006

I'm sitting in my kitchen, stunned, my hand still on the phone. I have just had a conversation on the phone with my sister that confirms, after all these years, what I have always suspected: she was much closer to my mother than I ever was. I know this now because my mother confided in Linda the secret of her life.

I had sent her the draft of the manuscript last week for her comments, and she called me this morning.

"I have to tell you something, but I don't know if I should," Linda began the conversation.

I was confused, and wondered if I had gotten some details wrong in the story.

"No, that's not it. There's just something that will make more sense to you if I tell you, but I promised Mom I would never tell you. She was afraid of what you would think of her."

"Well, now you have to tell me. Nothing is going to make me think less of her now."

"She really did have an affair with Uncle Jack." Linda blurted out.

Uncle Jack, you'll remember, was Sheila's father–Donna's friend who my mother saved in the fire.

"Are you sure? Maybe it was just a friendship–not a real affair," I offered.

"No, they went away together at least once. And he was always in New York when I was in the hospital and Mom was there alone. He divorced his wife hoping that Mom would leave Dad – but she never did."

Strangely, although I'm taken aback, I am not surprised. I had no idea at the time about the affair, but had been a witness to my parents' arguments and to my father's coldness over the years. I suspected there were many years without so much as a kiss between them.

My mother had needed, and found, a kindred spirit that gave her some of the understanding and affection she couldn't get from my father. And, I have to say, I'm glad she didn't live her life without it. I also now have an idea why I could never settle for a passionless marriage. Kids know everything you never tell them.

Following the crash, both Linda and Donna's friend Sheila were in the hospital for months recovering. Although my father was devoted to Linda, he hated hospitals, and did not often go. My mother, alone, talked Linda through the painful debridement of dead tissue, waited for her to wake up after she underwent skin grafts and held her hand when she came out of anesthesia sick and vomiting. She was strong when Linda needed her, but afterward, she fell apart, exhausted and spent.

Uncle Jack was visiting his daughter Sheila in the hospital at the same time that Linda was being treated that first year. So that is when their relationship started, Linda tells me. He was the one who was there for my mother, to pick up the pieces.

Linda says that it went on for years. Jack would come to the hospital to be with my mother even long after Sheila was released, and during the intermittent years that Linda was back in for surgeries. It makes sense that he would move to our neighborhood, that he would join our swim club to be close to my mother when she would be there for whole days in the summer with us.

As we talk, Linda reminds me about the day, when I was 7 or 8, that Jack's wife, also named Florence, appeared at our door. I wasn't alarmed to see her, and let her in as usual. But, when she saw my mother at the top of the stairs, she started railing at her.

"Leave my husband alone! I know what you are up to! Admit it!"

My father came out of the kitchen and grabbed the offending Florence and showed her out the door. He turned to me, watching it all from the landing, and said "Crazy! She's just a crazy lady!" I didn't understand much of what was said then, but finally my mother folded up into herself and fainted at the top of the stairs. Then, my father was standing over her yelling, "Get up, Florence! Don't do this–just get up!" When she continued to lay still, he picked her up and helped her to their room.

Uncle Jack continued to be in our lives. My father always bristled whenever he was around, but I don't know if he ever really knew the truth for sure. Uncle Jack doted on Linda and I and gave us gifts over the years that were outside the realm of what my father could afford. One year it was bicycles, the next it was one of the new remote control TVs for our room. Each time, my father threatened to give back the gifts, but my mother always talked him into letting us keep them.

After my father died, I ventured to ask my mother why she stayed with my father. We were sitting in her room at the assisted living apartment and she was sitting up in bed. I was holding her hand.

"He was my best friend in the world," she told me. "We had been through so much together."

After she died, I found another letter that was both a confirmation of my parents' troubled and complex marriage and a clue to my own restlessness. My mother wrote it when they were both well into their 70's and I don't know if she ever gave it to my father.

Al,
I never feel any attention from you…we appear to be roommates to the outside world. I'm sorry you've fallen out of love with me. My love and devotion have not changed, but I simply can't take your indifference. You may feel you are doing your duty, but without some demonstration of love, it doesn't matter. We have a few years left and truthfully I don't want to continue living them out in this fashion. Maybe it's time to separate.

Chapter Sixty
JANUARY 22, 1952
The Crash

4:00 PM

Parts of Linda's body were red and blistered. Other parts were black, white, brown and leathery, with precious few spots of healthy pink skin. Second and third-degree burns covered 80% of her small body.

Paramedics took great care with her, believing she was near death, moving her gently to a stretcher and into the ambulance. They tried to start an IV, but they couldn't find a vein. Her best chance was to get her to the Emergency Room.

In the ER, nurses and doctors were swift and practiced in assessing Linda's injuries. She was intubated to be sure she could breathe. Her eyes were examined for burns, and none were found. A catheter was inserted to measure urine output. Nurses started an IV after locating a usable vein in her leg to immediately begin replacing fluids.

A nurse urgently reported burns around Linda's torso and chest, a major concern. Burned tissue constricts as it settles and dries and could stop Linda's chest from rising and falling to take a breath, suffocating her. The tissue needed to be cut. A surgical cut, an escharectomy, was made to decrease the pressure.

Dead, burnt tissue was removed or cut away as much as possible. No ointments or dressings were applied at first, and Linda was covered with clean sheets and a blanket for warmth.

An oxygen tent was erected around her bed to promote healing of her skin, to protect against infection and to retain as much fluid as possible.

Later that night, nurses dressed Linda's wounds with silver sulphurdiazine and gauze to prevent infection. Being bathed for debridement (taking off dead skin) and changing her dressings was so painful that they gave her anesthesia for the ordeal. Later, my father gave the U.S. Atomic Commission permission to experiment with a new medication, called Tryptar, which was sprayed over her open burns to dry dead tissue.

Chapter Sixty-One
JANUARY 23, 1952
The Morning After

My father arrived at the hospital just as several ambulances turned in to the emergency room. He got the attention of the receptionist at the desk and explained that his wife and daughter were in the plane crash.

"They are both being treated right now Mr. Mandel," a nurse came to tell him. "It's best that you wait here and I'll let you know when they are admitted and where they will be."

It was two hours before anyone came out to talk to him again, telling my father what room my mother was in, and that Linda was in the Intensive Care Unit on the fourth floor. He'd have to wait awhile to see either of them. The nurse pointed him to another waiting room.

At two a.m., my father was sitting alone in the dimly lit hospital lounge when a nun quietly approached. With an arm on his shoulder, she told him that they had found Donna's body among the last of the victims excavated from the ashes.

His last vestige of hope gone, my father walked to a water fountain and took a long drink.

"Do you want some coffee or something Al," the nun asked.

"Not now sister, I want to see my family."

A photographer following the story intercepted my father at this juncture. The muscles around his eyes seemed to have let go, his mouth slack, his cheeks hostage to gravity with a weight too heavy to carry. The face of a soul's pain.

This Is Day He Must Tell Wife Child Died

Continued from Page 3

she yelled, "darling hurry, hurry" and started to go to her when a man grabbed her arm and pulled her out of the building.

"I just couldn't tell her that

Post Photo by Mellor

ALBERT MANDEL

Faces difficult task

Finally, my father was told he could go in and see Linda, but that my mother was sleeping and he should not disturb her. He felt relieved to postpone that next conversation with my mother, grateful to give her a few more oblivious hours.

He went up to see Linda in Intensive Care. At the door to the unit, he looked from bed to bed trying to find her. Finally, a nurse came over and led him to her.

He wouldn't have known it was his little girl, wrapped in bandages that circled her small face and mummified her torso and arms. She appeared as a small lump of cloth beneath the semi-transparent walls of the oxygen tent. Only her eyes were visible. She was surrounded by monitors and IV's with several tubes coming in and out of her body.

So tiny, my father thought. How can her little body withstand all this? He pled with God: Take me instead. Give this ordeal to me, and let her be.

Believing for a moment that his prayer might be answered, my father closed his eyes to wait for his transformation but was snapped back to reality by the bustle of nurses checking Linda's vital signs.

When a doctor walked in, my father approached him.

"Is she going to be alright?" he asked.

"I wish I could tell you more," the doctor said. "We're doing everything we can. Her burns are extensive and she is struggling to breathe. I would say she has a 50/50 chance right now of surviving. I'm very sorry."

My father moved his chair as close as possible to Linda's bed and watched her chest rise and fall, sometimes forgetting to breathe himself. He didn't believe she would live, and felt guilty for that thought. He knew my mother would need him to be hopeful, to believe in Linda's recovery, especially after she knew about Donna. He would try.

Nuns filed in to sit next to the bed in shifts, clicking rosary beads as they prayed.

"She is very close to God now," one nun said to him.

A rabbi came in and sat with my father for a while, offering a prayer, and finally just an arm around his shoulder. A St. Jude medal, Sacred Heart medal and a Star of David rested on Linda's pillow just outside the oxygen tent. Looking at the pile, my father thought, "I'll take any help I can get from any God that will listen."

A nurse who came in during the night told my father to go home and get some rest.

"That would be a nice idea–if I had a home to go to," he tried to joke.

Finally, as morning settled in on the hospital routine, my father was told he could see his wife.

"What does she know?"

"Not very much."

He glanced over at Linda and saw she was still unconscious.

Walking slowly to the elevator, he paused before pushing the button, turned around and leaned hard against the wall, trying to come up with some reason not to tell my mother that Donna was dead. How could he tell a mother the kind of news he has to tell his wife? It was impossible to find the words.

Seeing my mother awake and whole in her hospital bed, my father was overwhelmed with emotion. She leaned up on her pillow and gave him a weak smile.

He needn't have worried about the words. One look into his eyes, and my mother's worst fears were confirmed. He leaned over the bed to gently hug her and began to weep.

Chapter Sixty-Two **1980**

On New Year's Day, Linda and her live-in boyfriend, Tom, had argued and he took off with her house and car keys. He had recently moved in with her and her girls; five-year-old Debbie and six-year-old Cheryl. On the phone from Florida, she told me he was drinking again and was nearly hysterical as she recounted the scene – frantic about what to do. Stranded in the house with her daughters, she said she had no one else to call for help.

My parents lived only 10 miles from her, but she called me, 1,350 miles away in Connecticut.

I didn't really know what I would do when I got there, but I quickly found a non-stop flight. When I arrived, my sister was still in her bathrobe, her makeup smeared from wearing it through the night. The red-brown scars on her neck stood out in relief against her too-white make-up. Her eyes dripped black around red edges. Tears had cut paths down both cheeks. I felt a familiar ache at seeing her. The same ache that kept me away for long periods of time over the years.

Debbie and Cheryl seemed dazed – mute in front of the TV until they recognized me at the door.

"Aunt Judy, Aunt Judy!" they greeted me in unison. "Mommy, Aunt Judy is here!"

Linda and I needed only a few seconds to update me on the situation before I knew what I had to do. I loaded my two nieces of quickly into my red compact rental car.

"Mommy's not feeling too well," I told them. "You guys can visit with Grandma and Grandpa while I go get her some medicine." I turned on the radio and we sang along for the drive to my parents' condo. Then, I went looking for Tom at his favorite haunt by the beach.

Benny's on the Beach was a weathered white wood protrusion on the pier, jutting out over the ocean. An outside bar, sporting blue and white painted picnic tables, opened for drinks at noon. Along one side of the building was a patio of white plastic tables and chairs, scum-green umbrellas hawking Heineken and Coors Light. Smells of coffee, smoke and bacon mixed with the salty air.

Tom was hunkered inside with a cigarette and a cup of coffee. I watched him sweep back his oily black hair from his eyes with his fingers, rub his black and white beard stubble. He wore a wrinkled once-white tee shirt under his denim jacket. The blue of his jeans was dulled by brown shadow. He actually waved when he saw me.

He reminded me of another boyfriend Linda had in high school. When she brought home Vinny one night, my father had a visceral reaction to him. He recoiled when they shook hands. I heard a lot about it through my parents' bedroom wall.

"How old is he anyway," my father started. "He looks 30!"

We didn't know where Linda had met him, but my parents suspected it had something to do with the late nights out with her new girlfriend, that they may have been using fake ID's to go to bars.

My father also had an inkling that Vinny was an alcoholic and he set a trap for him. He told Linda to invite him over for dinner one evening. Then, he carefully left out his best Chivas Regal scotch. Vinny didn't stop drinking until he passed out on our couch. We never saw him again.

Even looking this disheveled, Tom acted like he owned the place and called all the waitresses "sweetheart" and "honey." I watched as they winced and rolled their eyes.

"How much to leave my daughter alone?" my father would have offered.

I had only one thing to say to him. "Give me my sister's keys and then go away."

Tom flashed crooked stained teeth and exhaled smoke in my face.

"You think you know her, but she's different now. She's not the sweet innocent big sister she makes herself out to be."

I already knew that just by looking at him. He embodied everything that made me fearful for my sister.

Linda once told me, "I can see the good in anyone."

It sounded like a positive thing at the time. Now, I wasn't so sure.

Even sitting here, at this awful juncture, I tried to find the good in this man. There must be moments, I told myself, that he gave her some measure of comfort, happiness, pleasure. Moments she deserved. This softened me toward him, at least enough to stop me from strangling him right there in Benny's.

Tom continued to try to talk me out of loving my sister.

"She lies to you all the time. About money. About who she takes up with at the bar. Hell, she lied to you for me when I needed some cash."

He returned her trust with total betrayal. He didn't understand that my love for my sister did not depend on her actions or choices. That nothing would change it. To me, she was still the vulnerable little girl with the scars who was looking for acceptance in any way she could, and I forgave her anything in its pursuit. I knew she could be taken advantage of by creeps like Tom, and I still wanted to protect her if I could.

I listened and nodded for an hour and a half. Finally, he gave up the keys.

Chapter Sixty-Three
JANUARY 25TH, 1952

In her mind, my mother moved a leg, an arm, but when she looked down, they were cemented to the mattress. An ache began in her chest and rested heavily in her arms, radiating out to her fingertips. She could not lift her head.

Her doctor said she was not physically injured, other than the minor burns on her hands, but that her feelings were common.

"Mothers who lose a young child often describe that kind of ache," the doctor explained to her. "Some say it's an ache to hold the child that has been lost."

I don't want to wake up, she thought.

But she still had one daughter that needed her. So she mustered her energy and tried on a hopeful attitude to face her little girl.

Walking into Linda's room, my mother took a deep breath. A scent, a foreign odor, settled in her nostrils. Antiseptic, pungent – undertones of burnt flesh.

The smell told her more than any doctor's words.

Linda was awake after a night and day of lurking in and out of consciousness. She must be in considerable pain, my mother thought.

A nurse began to change the bedding and Linda surprised her by shouting in the Hungarian accent she had picked up from her Grandma Schlesinger:

"I don't vant nobody to touch me!"

Seeing my mother, the nurse nodded and left.

Propped up in the bed, Linda lifted herself toward my mother.

"Mommy!"

"I'm here, sweetheart. You're ok. You're going to be ok. I love you."

Looking for a spot on Linda's body where she might make physical contact, my mother found none. Not a space to hold, to comfort her baby.

"I'm here," she repeated–her voice her only offering.

She studied Linda's body, noting the placement of each bandage, each scorched piece of skin, as Linda also searched my mother's face for answers. What happened to me–why does it hurt so much–what will happen now?

In one heroic lurch, Linda pulled herself up to be closer to her and my mother gasped, automatically reached out, but held herself in check.

Linda's left ear had dropped away and lay like a crisp piece of bacon on her pillow.

Chapter Sixty-Four
1980

Farmland, corn and cows surrounded the tiny airstrip lined with small planes. Steven and I lined up with the rest of the first time jumpers on the field as the sky diving coach explained how we would be trained over the next four hours.

I looked over at Steven and smiled. I had coerced him into this escapade. Our marriage was also hovering in the ethers, searching for some solid ground. He had returned home, and we were giving our marriage another try. When I mentioned that I had met some skydivers recently and thought I'd like to try it, we planned to do it together as a kind of launch to our new life. The plan had ignited new excitement between us. It seemed like we were back in our element, embarking on the kind of adventure that first brought us together. I held out some hope for the day, and for us.

Our training consisted of climbing 12 steps to the raised platform, then – jump, bend, roll, jump, bend, roll. Over and over and over and over.

"Don't keep your knees locked, you need to stay loose or you'll break your legs!" my trainer yelled on my first practice jump.

By the time we boarded the plane, I'd taken around 20 practice jumps, but locked my knees on 19 of them. I was nervous about jumping from 3,000 feet.

Part of our training was to pack our own parachutes, so we clamored into the packing room and took our places around a rough wooden table that extended the length of the room. One of the trainers took me aside. He had watched me take my fateful practice falls, and had taken a liking to me. He didn't want to see me break apart on impact, he said, and handed me an extra large chute.

"Listen," he whispered. "For your height and weight, you should land like a butterfly."

I saw Steven watching our interchange suspiciously, but nodded him an "ok."

We were among four passengers in the white Cessna 182, all laden with parachutes, getting ready to taxi up the runway, reach altitude and then jump out. The wind was still. The proximity of danger, the possibility of death, the fear and adrenaline had its usual effect on me – an inexplicable high. And, it suddenly reminded me of my parents. I hadn't told them about my jumping from an airplane. I didn't want them to worry, or to try to talk me out of it.

If abject fear had a face, I saw it reflected in each one of my parachute-laden companions. We had just enough time to question our sanity and say a short prayer during our ascent. Soon, two jumpers had disappeared into the blue, their shouts fading as they fell away from us. A quiet hollow between jumps. Steven looked calm just before he stepped off into the sky. I had a sinking feeling I might never see him again.

"Judy, you're up–stand over here in the door. One, two ---GO!" SHOVE–WHAM–OUT.

A static line opened my chute automatically after three seconds – a detail that has probably saved thousands of lives for first-time jumpers. Mine for sure. I never considered pulling my chute once I was floating in the sky.

You're supposed to immediately look up at your parachute to be sure it has deployed properly. If it is twisted or has a hole in it, you need to quickly pull your reserve. This too, we practiced for four hours.

I never looked up.

The euphoria of floating in air was so complete, all I could think was, "How beautiful, how silent, how awesome, look at all the little houses." A frozen frame of blue and white held me between the earth and sky.

The radio strapped to my belly startled me when it started yelping.

"Judy, Judy, come in, Judy. Are you there, Judy? Please reply, Judy. You're doing fine–pull your right cord a little bit. Now the left a little. You're doing good–coming right into the target area."

As the ground zoomed up to meet me, I thought, "Don't lock your goddamn knees."

I landed softly, thanks to that extra large chute, and was endorphined out of my mind by the thrill. About 30 yards away I saw a group of people huddled around someone. I unhooked my chute and ran over to see that Steven was still on the ground. He hadn't landed well, and his six-foot frame didn't help. Something in my stomach lurched. If he was hurt, it was my fault, my idea to do this crazy thing. After about a minute he was able to get up with my help – to the applause of the crowd.

It turned out that this was our last adventure together. The excitement of the jump soon wore off and we were grounded once again. The gap between us widened, and I began to feel a disturbingly familiar emptiness.

We went to several marriage counselors who managed to get us to unearth our feelings of resentment and hurt. Steven felt rushed into the marriage and unable to pursue his own dreams. I felt neglected and punished. I thought of how my mother suffered from my father's neglect over the years, and I was haunted by his rejection of me in so many small ways as a child. I was determined not to live my adult life with that kind of misery.

We didn't fight, because that was not the nature of our relationship. Instead, we discussed it all until we started to realize there was nothing to be done.

Chapter Sixty-Five
2006

Justin and I are on our way to Paris. A trip I've promised him for years. I made the arrangements for this trip before remembering it would be my mother's one-year yarest and I wouldn't be home to light her memorial candle, let it burn the full 24 hours, hear her name called or say the *Kaddish* at Temple.

He's taken three years of French now, and plans to practice the language on our trip. I'm sure he'll run circles around me in that department. I think we are both looking forward to this trip for just the two of us. His life has gotten busy with friends and we don't spend the time together that we used to.

When he was little and I was struggling to pay the rent, Friday was our special night. After work, I'd pick him up from daycare and take him to a local pizza place that had games and rides for kids. It was the treat of our week, that I could afford. It was literally the cost of a $5.00 small pizza and a few dollars for games. Those nights were good for both of us, not going back to our tiny apartment like every other night of the week, and seeing my little boy laugh while we played air hockey together.

Now, I stop dead still in the busy corridor, realizing that we're leaving from the same Newark Airport that Captain Reid tried to reach on January 22, 1952.

"Mom, come on, we'll miss our plane," Justin, now 18, pulls on my arm.

His low voice startles me and he towers over me. Until yesterday his hair was down to his shoulders in some kind of nonconformist solidarity, but now he has a head full of brown curls that let me see his wonderful blue eyes. The haircut was a break with his younger self–one step closer to recreating himself for his future.

On April 5th, the anniversary of my mother's death, although I am far from home I find a place that feels right to me to light a candle. We enter Notre Dame and I feel a quiet awe. Whispered prayers echo in the cavernous cathedral, bouncing off the ancient pillars, swirling against the stained glass in a prayer-soup. It doesn't matter that our religion doesn't match. It's the spirit here that I know my mother would understand.

I make my way to a long table of candles. I note the suggested donation and take out some coins to put in the box. Justin is walking ahead of me but when he sees me take a candle, he comes to stand beside me. I close my eyes, light the candle and whisper "I miss you, Mom."

* * *

Last night, the dream was so real that I woke empty and tired. It was my mother. There so fully I could smell her perfume; the powdery scent of lilacs. I could touch her hair; thin, fragile. I could feel her lightest kiss on my cheek.

She was holding on. Needing to let go.

I sensed her being pulled, nearly dragged away. She grasped at the edges of me. Through her eyes I saw a blue, swirling vortex. Sucking at her, ripping her from me, then – gone.

Chapter Sixty-Six
1953
THE IDEA OF ME

My father thumbed through his wallet while he waited in the small examining room. He rubbed his eyes with the palms of his hands, and had almost finished counting the number of floor tiles when Dr. Berger appeared. Clutching a chart in one hand, the doctor shook my father's hand with the other. They had known each other for many years now, through the birth of two children–the death of one.

A small dark-haired man with a kind, round face, Dr. Berger was a family doctor that still made house calls. His black bag held both lollipops and penicillin. He would take an IOU or a chicken dinner when you couldn't pay.

"It's good to see you, Al. You look well–what can I do for you?"

"It's not me. I'm worried to death about Florence. She doesn't want to go out, or even get dressed unless it's to do something for Linda. Even now, after all this time. She cries all the time and sleeps whenever she can."

"You know, Al, women take these things differently than us. I know you–you just keep busy working–right?" Dr. Berger slid the chart under his arm, reached into his jacket pocket for a prescription pad and scribbled a name and number.

"Call this doctor–Dr. Horowitz. He's a friend, and a lontzman. Make an appointment for you and Florence to go together. He's a psychiatrist–he may be able to help."

"A psychiatrist? But she's not crazy, doc–just not herself. You really think we need a head shrinker–and both of us?"

"I think it may help Al," Dr. Berger answered.

My father took the note, though, and agreed to give it a try.

* * *

"Dr. Berger suggested we go see this Dr. Horowitz," he told my mother after dinner that night.

"Why, who is he–what for?" She didn't turn around from washing the dishes in the sink.

My father was grateful she had her back to him. "I told him how you are–staying in bed, not wanting to go out, crying all the time. He's worried about you. Dr. Horowitz is a psychiatrist. I think we should try it, Flurry."

My mother agreed to go, and was inwardly thankful. She put up a good front for Linda, especially when she needed her, but she would collapse in private and had no energy for anything else. My mother felt that if it wasn't for Linda's care, she would have no reason to keep living. It was taking a toll on her and sooner or later it would affect Linda. If she wasn't strong for her, Linda could never get through what lay ahead–of that she felt sure. My father kept the family on an even keel, but my mother felt she was the only one with the fortitude to be there for Linda when she was scared, when she was hurting, when she needed encouragement to get up and walk after surgery. That motivation gave her a reason to tend to herself, and to agree to see Dr. Horowitz.

The next week, my parents went to see Dr. Horowitz after my father got out of work. His office was a second floor walk-up in a red brick office building on East Jersey Street. It was a cozy room with three overstuffed blue cloth chairs and a well-worn brown leather sofa. A small table held some magazines and a box of tissues. The doctor had his oak desk in the corner of the room.

"Sit anywhere you like," Dr. Horowitz offered, extending his hand to greet my parents. He was tall and lanky with black graying hair and a five o'clock shadow beginning to hallow his cheeks.

"What brings you here today?"

My father explained about the crash, losing Donna, Linda's injuries.

"We're really here because I'm worried about Florence. But, ya know doc, maybe it just takes time–maybe Florence will get back to herself in a little while."

At that, my mother put her head down, clasped her hands in her lap and let out a heavy sigh.

"What is it, Florence?" Dr. Horowitz asked.

"It's just that Al expects me to get back to normal. And normal is gone. Donna is gone, Linda is so hurt–I won't get back to myself. The person he wants me to be again is gone. There is a part of me that will never come back."

Anger discharged between them, quick as a shot, silent as a glance.

Dr. Horowitz let them take a moment, then offered,

"Al, I don't think it's a matter of wanting or not wanting. It isn't something Florence can just decide to get over. It's not unusual for her to feel that she's lost a piece of herself."

"I was there too, ya know, doc. Donna was my daughter, too," my father muttered.

"I never said I was the only one suffering through this," my mother said. "I just think we are different people and I am not bouncing back as quickly as Al wants me to."

"Everyone grieves a little differently, and it's important to respect that," Dr. Horowitz said.

"I just don't know how you can do such normal things again, jumping right back into the life you had before everything changed," my mother said to my father.

"What would you have me do? I can't just sit around thinking about things and making it worse."

"It's probably Al's way of coping. His way to keep maintaining the family–to keep providing," Dr. Horowitz interjected.

This is the only way I know to keep going. Otherwise I will just fold into myself – like you have decided to do!"

My father's jaw firmly clenched, a serious scowl overtook his face.

My mother's eyes softened, and she reached for his hand. My father saw the path of his wife's tears through her makeup, running down her neck, pooling in a dark stain on her white collar.

"I think I do understand," he said quietly, seeing her pain.

"I'm not going to mince words," Dr. Horowitz continued. "Many couples have a very rough time after losing a child and many get divorced. I don't want that to happen here. They blame themselves, or worse, they may blame each other."

"Have you two thought of having another child? Many couples that have lost children find that having another helps them heal."

"I don't know," my father said. "It seems like we'd be tempting fate, after what's happened to our girls. Maybe this is how it's meant to be."

"What about you, Florence?" the doctor asked.

"Maybe it would help. I always wanted two children at least. All I see now is struggle ahead. And it might be good for Linda to have a sister or brother. Maybe take the focus off of her and her problems somewhat. Another baby could give us all back a sense of a normal life–a normal family again."

The prescription, then, for their own survival was a child conceived to heal the family. Untouched, they thought, by their tragedy. And, with another mission – to live life large for them all – to ride the biggest waves, and carry them on her wake.

Chapter Sixty-Seven 1953 PRESCRIPTION FILLED

In his heart, my father wasn't at all sure they should have another child. He missed his little girl terribly–was bitter about her death. He blamed himself for not being there to protect his family. He replayed his revised scene in his mind a thousand times: my mother rushing out of the apartment with Linda rolled in the quilt while he ran back to push the beam off of Donna, lifting her up over the flames and smoke, carrying her down the steep stairway just before it collapsed.

There could be no replacement for Donna. He didn't want one. And he thought Linda would need their undivided attention for many years.

But, he wanted his wife back. He needed her smiling again. If a new baby would do it, he would comply.

My father chose the Blumenkrantz Hotel in Lakewood because he knew how much his wife loved the ocean, and because it was an affordable way to get away to the beach for a few days. They needed a change of scenery. Different surroundings to shift their perspective, lift their spirits–their souls–from the oppressive daily grind.

"A perfect beach day Flurry!" my father declared as they pulled in to the hotel parking lot. Entering the lobby, my mother took in the wood paneling, the leather upholstery, the Victorian grandeur of the place. She noted the indoor pool, adjacent to the formal dining room. Her hope for the weekend was renewed. Until now, she had been doubtful, but she didn't show it for my father's sake.

She knew he was more fragile than he let on. She remembered the night his claustrophobia kicked in as they rode through the Lincoln tunnel to New York City. They were stuck in traffic in the tunnel for 45 minutes. An endless black netherworld. Suddenly, my father couldn't catch his breath and was hyperventilating–he said he couldn't breathe at all. My mother took his hand and calmed him. She talked to him about their plans for the next day and told him when to take a breath. They would breathe each breath together until they got through the tunnel.

They checked in to the hotel, unpacked their suitcases, changed into bathing suits and headed for the beach. My mother wore her black one-piece suit, cut in an octagonal shape at the top with a small tasteful skirt at the bottom. My father was in his only green and blue plaid bathing trunks. His boney white chest screamed for a sunburn.

They drove to Bradley Beach and picked a spot midway between the water and the boardwalk to lay their hotel towels out next to each other.

"We should've brought an umbrella," my father said, squinting. "The sun is so strong today, no clouds to block it at all."

At that, my mother dug into her beach bag and produced two hats. A Yankees baseball cap for him and a floppy brimmed canvas one for herself.

My father smiled, leaned over and kissed his wife on the cheek. "That's why I married you –you're always taking care of us."

My mother reached her arm over his shoulder and gave him a squeeze, "I try."

"What other hazari *do you have in that bag? A hot dog maybe? Some mustard and a coke? How about one of those big salty pretzels?"*

"Now you're making me hungry," my mother slapped him on the chest.

They left their towels and walked to the boardwalk, bringing back hot dogs and cokes and two big pretzels.

"This isn't helping me keep my girlish figure," my mother said, taking a bite of pretzel.

"Me neither," my father said seriously. He stood and posed, hands on his hips, tilting his chin to the sky. Looking at his skinny physique, my mother burst out laughing, nearly spitting out her mouthful of coke. Suddenly, she was uncontrollable. Shaking, laughing–tears streaming. She put down her soda and folded her arms in on herself, to hold herself together. My father was momentarily stunned, but knelt next to her to put his arms around her to calm her down. He instinctively pulled her toward him.

Their hats had fallen off and lay in the sand and their hotdogs were getting cold. My parents found themselves in an unexpected embrace, holding each other tightly, neither one willing to be the first to let go.

Chapter Sixty-Eight MAY 21, 1954

When my mother first went to the doctor suspecting she was pregnant, he told her she was wrong.

"Florence, I know how much you want a baby, but you're just not pregnant. The urinalysis shows up negative. Your symptoms may be a hysterical pregnancy. Sometimes when a woman wants so much to have a baby, her body mimics pregnancy."

But, by then my mother knew that doctors were people–not gods. They made mistakes and had different opinions. She knew she was pregnant and went to a new doctor.

At 38, she was an older mother–especially by 1950's standards. Against her doctor's recommendation, she insisted on being awake and un-medicated for the delivery.

"I'm not going to miss a minute of it. I don't care about the pain," she told my father. "I want to be fully aware during the whole thing. After all we've been through, I don't think I would believe it if I was put to sleep and woke up with a new baby."

After the delivery, the last thing my mother heard before she passed out was "Oh boy!" So, when she woke up, she told my father, "We had a little boy Al–you've got the son you wanted!"

"I don't think so!" my father said.

My father had just seen me in the nursery in my little pink cap with the pink ribbon on my name card that read: "Mandel, Baby Girl." The doctor told him everything went well, that his baby girl was healthy and his wife fine.

"I'm absolutely thrilled to have another little girl," my father assured her, and presented her with a clear blue 2 kt. diamond, commemorating the birth. Later, he designed a new wedding ring for her around the nearly perfect stone.

Chapter Sixty-Nine
May 22, 1954

My mother's breasts were full. She longed to hold her new baby to her, to help her learn to suck, to feel the relief of the release of her milk.

A nurse brought the baby and helped position the newborn in the crook of my mother's left arm. The baby seemed disinterested until she coaxed her to take the nipple, then she reached a tiny hand out of her blanket. My mother relaxed at the familiar feeling, the tingle that reached into her womb. As the baby became more intent, gurgling and smacking, my mother's tears mingled with her milk.

The nurse came closer and laid a hand lightly on her shoulder.

"She's so much like my first," my mother told her. "The way she reaches up, the sound she makes, the crinkle in her forehead when she eats."

It was the only time my mother would breastfeed me. Trying once more, she found herself tense at the baby's touch, her milk refusing to come. The visceral connection to her first, lost child was too much for her body to accommodate. By the time she left the hospital, she had taken medication to dry her milk.

Chapter Seventy
2006

I am shocked to notice that it's dark outside and I've been working into the night. David is working late, and I'm alone in the house. I feel that I'm coming to the end of this project, with more understanding of my role in my family and how a plane crash before I was born effected my path.

The realization that I was a replacement for Donna has given my life a new dimension, and I finally feel grateful that I could help my family heal from that devastating tragedy. Working through the layers of my childhood, I have some long sought answers about how my father's attitude toward me shaped my choices and relationships with men. And I know that my father loved me the best he could.

Coming to an end is a bittersweet feeling. When I'm really done, I will finally be leaving my family's tragedy behind me. I've turned over each stone and looked into every closet. Like shining a flashlight underneath a bed, the now illuminated ghosts can't get to me.

I won't leave behind my parents though. They still live in my head. Their voices, their faces are still clear to me. Even more so now that I understand them as the complex people they were. My walls are still covered with their pictures. I've decided to keep them up in my office. But I'll take down the crash scenes, the headlines, the photos in the hospital. The ones I'll keep on the bulletin board are the happier times; at our home in Cranford when my mother would serve the biggest turkey we'd ever seen, or at the beach together, or my parents dancing – always the cha cha.

Chapter Seventy-One **1981**

I lingered at home in the morning, nearly missing my flight to Florida. When my alarm went off, John pulled me back to the warm bed, not wanting me to leave him. He never wanted me to leave him. The need left me weak, and trapped me there.

"Don't go. You don't have to. I mean, you aren't doing the surgery yourself are you?"

"It's my father, of course I have to go."

My father was having heart bypass surgery, and I was flying to Florida to be with him and my mother and Linda. John seemed to have no understanding of my need to be there. I knew then that this second try at marriage was failing – I was failing – again. Free-falling in this belly flop of a marriage that was wearing me out.

We met when I had just gone back to college to get my degree. I was singing and playing guitar nights and weekends to pay for tuition. Steven and I were still married, but our sexual hiatus was wearing as thin as the knees in my old jeans. He had completely stopped coming to my singing jobs.

So, it had begun with John's eyes – bottomless brown – finding mine from a table in the back of the bar where I played guitar. It was like pulling a loose thread on a sweater. Scorching me with hard, blatant questions and hungry, intoxicating answers.

He was the opposite of Steven in so many ways. Dark, warm with a hearty laugh and a gang of friends always around him. His longish near-black hair hung into his eyes. The drooping mustache collected a whisp of white foam from his beer.

He followed me from Happy Hour to a later club gig and brought his entourage to fill the place. He silently unraveled cords, set up my amp, plugged in my guitar, sent up drinks while I played. He even lugged it all out to my car at 2 am. In the dark, deserted parking lot, he took me by the shoulders and leaned into me.

"I'm married," I pulled away.

"But are you happy?" It was a trap-door question that I couldn't answer.

"Your eyes look very sad, " he said. "At least meet me for lunch tomorrow. Just to talk."

Our trysts started innocently enough. He told me about his advertising firm and showed me some of his newest work – an ad for sealant, a brochure for a tool company. We talked about my writing class and I brought him some of my work to discuss. We were just friends, I told myself for a while. But soon I didn't pull away when he reached for me and our lunches ended in his bed each time.

I found I couldn't lie to my husband, who had first been my best friend. I was no good at sneaking around, taking secret phone calls, making excuses. So pretty quickly, I left the husband for the lover – thinking "isn't that the right thing?" John helped me find a part of myself, that at 27, I thought was lost. And he was so unlike my father – so affectionate, so attentive, so demonstrative – that I was sure I would not repeat my fatal error of being attracted to the familiar chill. I was convinced that this new passion was my remedy, unaware that I was just playing the same song backwards. I would discover John had familiar insecurities, but that they manifested in his being overly controlling and jealous.

"Be careful what you wish for," my mother used to say.

In a matter of months after we were together, I realized I had merely exchanged the texture of my loneliness. This man could be my lover, but never my friend. He truly didn't care about my well being, but only as it affected him. He didn't support anything that could potentially take me away from him, for even a few hours. His jealousy infiltrated every part of our relationship.

He didn't show up for my graduation from college, something I had worked long and hard to achieve. When I got my first real job as a reporter, John called the bureau office at my story deadline each night.

"Are you really working? Who's there with you? When will you be home?"

He complained about the hours. He wanted me home. He wanted me to have dinner for him. He wanted sex every night. He ripped the phone from the wall when he thought I was getting calls from my ex and threw potatoes (uncooked) at me to get me off the phone. Friends were afraid for me. Then, I became afraid for myself. The stress finally manifested as actual illness with a flare-up of Crohn's disease and I finally couldn't ignore that I was emotionally, spiritually and physically miserable.

When I left him, John kept the expensive silk negligee he bought me, with the soft intricate black lace trim. He swore later that he burned it.

* * *

They waited for me. The expert on bypassing my father's heart. They wouldn't let them open him up until I arrived to wish him luck and maybe say goodbye. I didn't think they would do that for me.

"See Flurry, she made it!"

They wheeled my father down the hall and I walked in step with the squeak-squeak of the gurney wheels, holding his hand.

"I love you Dad."

He looked straight up at the dimpled ceiling tiles that folded quickly behind him and squeezed my hand.

"You too."

His words, his wet cheek, were a gift.

Chapter Seventy-One
APRIL 8, 1988

Bob and I were married for four years when I got pregnant, something we had hoped for. Justin's birth grounded me. Changed my chemical composition. A catalyst in the creation of new matter.

"You are perfect," I whispered to him, only hours old. "You will have what you need to grow strong, the life you deserve. You can count on me."

His face lit up when I sang to him –

"Hush little baby, don't say a word, mamma's gonna buy you a mockingbird."

His eyes followed me around the room, his smile collapsed when I left his room. But, even in the midst of mother-euphoria, I was aware of the precipitous cliff. The seeds of my parents' warnings fully blossoming.

Anything can happen.

Planes fall from the sky.

Returning from shopping, I imagined Justin's skull cracked like a watermelon on the pavement. I hallucinated fire engines and ambulances. Incinerated baby on the perfect lawn.

My mother's voice was often in my head:

"Only you will protect your own child. No one else will watch out for him like you."

But I also felt a swelling calm. Molecules of my mother's courage, her fortitude, crystallizing into a solid force. I was ready to run into a blazing building, fight to save even one finger.

A year later, my baby son was pressing his face into my neck, holding his ears. His body shook each time the planes roared overhead. We were watching an air show of jets, entranced by the swoops and dives.

They first flew in formation, the tips of their wings nearly touching. Dipping in fluid unison motion, the planes formed a perfect geometry of dark angles against blue.

The planes were sleek blue and yellow machines. Each Boeing F/A-18 Hornet was numbered brightly on the tail. We could see "U.S. Navy" emblazoned across the top of the wingspan when they turned topsy-turvy. Silhouette pilots could be seen inside the glass cockpits. The planes trailed white smoke as they soared and looped.

It was a painting of flight until one and then another broke away from the rest. Upside down, sideways, noses down losing altitude. Each aimed at ground zero.

"They never crash," I was assured.

I could barely keep still when the planes careened downward, then pulled up at the very last moment. I fought my instinct to turn and run, far and fast, my child fastened to my chest. Finally, though, the tempting of fate proved to be too much. I tugged at my husband's arm, pointed to our son, shook my head, headed for the exit. His eyes were a question, "What the…" But I was already gone. Clutching, running, panting. Breaking through the hot dog eating, beer-drinking crowd. Ignoring the oohs and ahhs elicited by the pilots' feats. Elbowing and pushing my way out to the clearing. Away from the impending wreckage.

Chapter Seventy-Three
1991

Bob had brought the mortgage papers to the hospital for me to sign, where I was recovering from a flare up of Crohn's just five months after Justin was born.

"I need you to sign these so we can put some more money into the house. It will increase the value. Trust me, it will be fine."

From the moment I met him, I trusted Bob. His calm assurance, his easy good looks. His sensitive eyes. We seemed well matched this time, and I was secure enough in our marriage to go ahead and have a child.

But only a few months after signing those loan papers, Bob lost another job and money was so tight that I had trouble paying for groceries.

For another two years I trusted that he could put our house of cards back together, scotch tape our credit, glue back together the splinters of our security. But, he gravitated to jobs that never quite worked out for him. Insurance sales, financial planning.

I was home alone most nights with the baby. When he was home, Bob busied himself in his workshop until I fell asleep. I was sure now that I was entirely unlovable, that this pattern of retreat was somehow my doing. I felt stranded on an island, afraid for our financial straits, without the comfort of a loving relationship as a buffer.

We drifted further and further from the life I promised my son when I first held him.

"I don't think I can do it," Bob finally told me on the way home from a therapy session.

His face was stark honesty; his eyes revealing a finality that closed my heart.

We postponed the inevitable split, but when the foreclosure sign was posted on the bluegrass of our perfectly mowed lawn, I scooped up my baby and ran before the burning cinders trapped us.

On moving day, our house grew smaller and smaller in my rearview mirror until it disappeared behind me. Beside me in his car seat, Justin suddenly looked as serious as a three-year old could get. His tiny brow furrowed in worry.

"When is daddy coming?"

It was a long mile before I could speak, to give him my practiced answer. The cliff was upon us and I was powerless to stop his fall, to stop his heart from breaking.

* * *

In a weird twist, this was one of the few times in my life that I did not feel guilty, that my life was somehow balanced with Linda's. Linda seemed to always have a hard time, either financially or with men. When my life was going well, I felt like it wasn't fair. This time, my struggle to maintain three jobs and feed my child seemed my due, and was what I deserved as the survivor, the one blessed – the replacement for the angel.

I was determined, though, that Justin wouldn't suffer for my failings. He truly was a force behind my landing a good job at a national insurance company, leading to a stable career in corporate communications for many years. It enabled me to buy the house I felt he deserved to grow up in, in a quiet suburban town –miles and miles from any airport.

Afterward

I'm sitting in my office looking out on the big maple tree in my front yard. The leaves have just changed to the bright yellow I wait for each year. Some are lying on the front lawn like decorations. It's a time of year I love here in Connecticut, and in my home where everyone who comes down this quiet street either lives here or is visiting someone.

As I revisit some of the toughest times of my life, it is from the distance and quiet of a place far removed from the turmoil. That tornado of marriage and divorce is finally over for me. I remember my younger self almost as an old friend, who gratefully has grown up and found her way. Who has somehow left behind the anger at a father who only did the best he could.

Ultimately it's understanding and forgiveness that heals. This journey into the past has yielded greater understanding of my parents and what they went through from the time of the crash until their deaths. I can't help but forgive them for anything either of them may have inadvertently done that hurt me. But, maybe most importantly for me, it has illuminated my own story for myself, helping me to understand the origins of many of my own issues that got in the way of my choosing the right partner and in making a relationship work. And, I'm able now to forgive myself for my own mistakes, and am able to love more fully.

Ultimately it's being known and accepted for myself, with all my past baggage and flaws, that has been the difference for me with David. And, finding a man secure enough in himself to let me be who I am and support my endeavors to be the best I can be.

Nothing happens in a vacuum, and I recognize the role that some counseling played along the way. Though, I have to say that no marriage counseling ever worked for me in my three failed marriages. But, the love of good friends made my metamorphosis possible. The friend who helped me move out in a rush, the friend who took me in when I had nowhere to go, the friends who helped move me from one place to another time and time again. You know who you are.

My son is now in college, grown into a sensitive, responsible young man with a mission to make the world a better place. He is indeed my shining star, and the reason I cannot be sorry for any path that led to his presence in my life.

My husband, David, is my best friend, my staunch supporter, my rock. I like to think it was not pure luck that brought us together, but some master plan that deemed we both finally deserved each other – deserved happiness. My father still played a role in my choice for a mate this time, but now it was his best traits I found in David–his humor, his responsibility, his honesty.

My sister, Linda, remains a big part of my life. Though she is far away in distance, she is never far from my thoughts. She still doesn't have an easy road. Still needs a knee replacement that makes it difficult for her to walk, and she is too afraid of possible amputation to have it done. She struggles to find the right medications to kill the chronic pain she still has. I try to do what I can, but feel it is never enough. Some feelings never change.

THE END

EPILOGUE 2009

Safe passage sister
Where your spirit, true and free
Is unencumbered.
Our parents welcome you.
Our sister greets you.
You marvel at the beauty
Of unimaginable colors on this earth,
At the music that emanates
From a soul's joy.
Wait for me.
Save a seat – as always –
For your little sister.

My sister Linda passed away on July 25, 2009 – on Donna's birthday. She was a heavy smoker for nearly 40 years and had lung cancer that closed her airway. In two weeks, she was gone. The last few years had been difficult for Linda, fighting to find relief from chronic pain from her faulty knee replacement, and resulting back pain. Still, she was positive about her future.

Even as she lay in ICU, intubated and unable to speak to me, I never for a moment believed that she would lose this battle. She never had. She was my brave sister who survived monumental challenges, and came out smiling and joking. It never crossed my mind that there could be a fight she would lose.

Just an hour before she died she was still looking out for me, writing a note asking me if I had gotten the answers I needed about her condition – to make me comfortable with what was happening. She joked with her daughters not to let me take her to Germany for treatment *like Farrah*. She also wrote her decision to be cremated *like Mommy, Daddy, Donna.* She had made the decision to accept this as her final chapter and her smile was peaceful.

Linda helped me a great deal with this book. I couldn't have written it without her help. She remembered all the details and answered my questions for over four years. She was able to help me choose the cover for the book just before she died.

ACKNOWLEDGEMENTS

Thank you first and foremost to my sister, Linda (Mandel) Driskell, for all of her knowledge and incredible memory – and mostly for her love. I miss you terribly.

My husband, David Schwartzer's love and support throughout this emotionally exhausting process was no less than saintly. Many times I would not have gone on with the project if not for his encouragement.

Enormous thanks are due to Anthony Valerio, teacher and mentor, whose patience with me was herculean and without whom I surely could not have completed this work. Thank you for your wisdom, knowledge and generosity.

Every new author should be so lucky as to have a sensitive and skilled editor like Rachel Sherman who helped me craft my story into a real book.

Thanks are due to my writing workshop pals who labored with me through each chapter and added valuable advice each time, including Jonathan Ricard, Carol Lyn Woodring and Brenda L. Planck, MD.

A special thanks to:
Justin Alexander Butler (my boy), for inspiration, editorial advice and encouragement always.

Deborah Cannarella for her advice, writing expertise and encouragement.

Susan Jorgensen for editing advice and inspiration.

Molly Rector, for editorial recommendations and advice.

Patricia Sheehy, who told me for many years that I should write this story, and didn't quit nagging me until I did it. She also helped me choose the title for the book and talked me through many issues.

Thank you to those who helped in my research, including:
Elizabeth firemen Al Trojanowicz and Gary Haszko;
Rabbi Jeffrey Bennett, Temple Sinai, Newington, Connecticut;
Dr. Richard Stone;
Anne Carroll, Esq.

And to friends, too numerous to name here, for their love and support.

REFERENCES

Newspapers:

The New York Times

The Elizabeth Daily Journal

The Star Ledger

Books:

The Bible (Old Testament)

Kolatch, Alfred J. The Jewish Book of Why. Middle Village, New York: Jonathan David Publishers, Inc., 2000

Didion, Joan. *The Year of Magical Thinking.* New York: Alfred A. Knopf, 2005

Finkbeiner, Ann K. *After the Death of a Child.* Baltimore, Maryland: The Johns Hopkins University Press, 1998.

Floyd, Gregory. *A Grief Un-Veiled.* Brewster, Massachusetts: Paraclete Press,1999.

Goodman, Sandy. *Love Never Dies.*San Diego, California: Jodere Group, Inc., 2001

Guggenheim, Bill & Judy. *Hello From Heaven!* New York: Bantam Books, 1997

Marx, Robert J. and Wengerhoff Davidson, Susan. *Facing the Ultimate Loss Coping with the Death of a Child.* Fredonia, Wisconsin: Champion Press, LTD, 2003.

McCracken, Anne and Semel, Mary. *A Broken Heart Still Beats After Your Child Dies.* Center City, Minnesota: Hazelden, 1998.

Rosof, Barbara D. *The Worst Loss, How Families Heal from the Death of a Child.* New York: Henry Holt and Company, An Owl Book, 1995.

Turner, Jean-Rae and Koles, Richard T. *Images of America: Elizabeth.* Great Britain: Arcadia, 1997.

Urdang, Laurence, editor. *The Timetables of American History.* New York: Simon & Schuster, 1996.

Internet Resources

Civil Aeronautics Board, *Accident Report*, File No. 1-0016, Released: April 28, 1952.

TIME ARCHIVE. *Last Flight.* Monday, February 04, 1952.

Arlington National Cemetery Website. Memorial page for Robert Porter Patterson, Captain, U.S. Army. *Former Secretary of War Robert P. Patterson, Combined Services Full Honor Funeral*, 22-25 January 1952.

Ancestry.com.

www.musckids.com/health_library/burns/secdeg.htm

www.ci.phoenix.az.us/FIRE/burns.html

www.vh.org/adult/patient/surgery/burnwoundcare

www.medicineau.net.au/clinical/surgery/Burns.html

www.burn-recovery.org/treatment.htm

www.ncbi.nlm.nih.gov

www.stjoehospital.com/burn

Footnote

1. *Mourning and Melancholia*, Sigmund Freud, 1917